EXPERIMENTS IN RELIEF PRINT MAKING

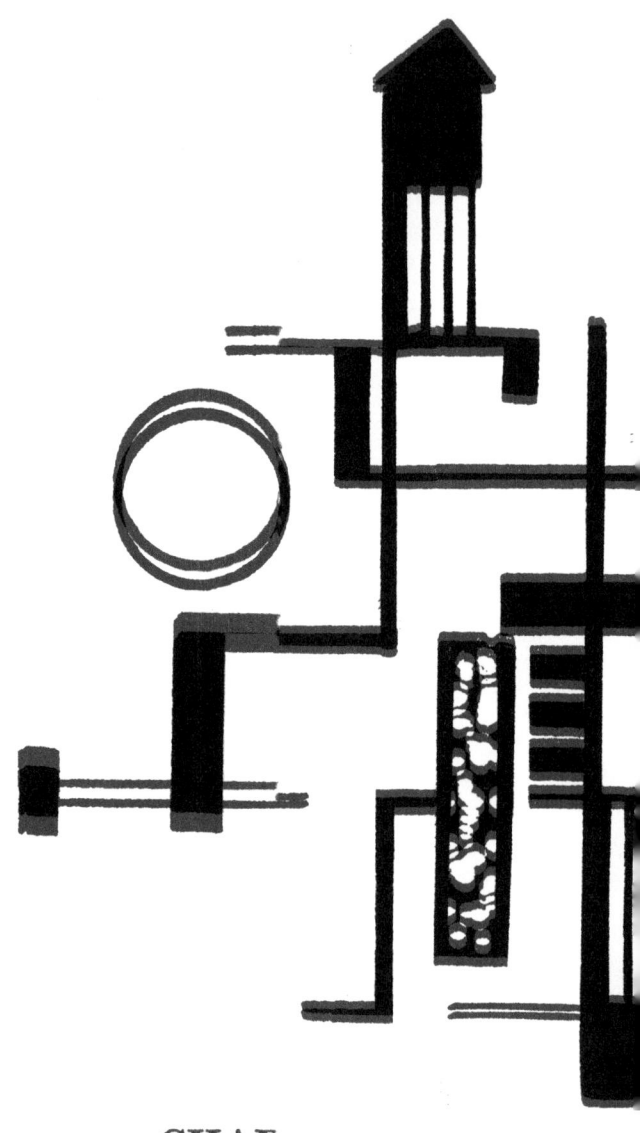

CHARLES SMITH
EXPERIMENTS IN RELIEF
1954

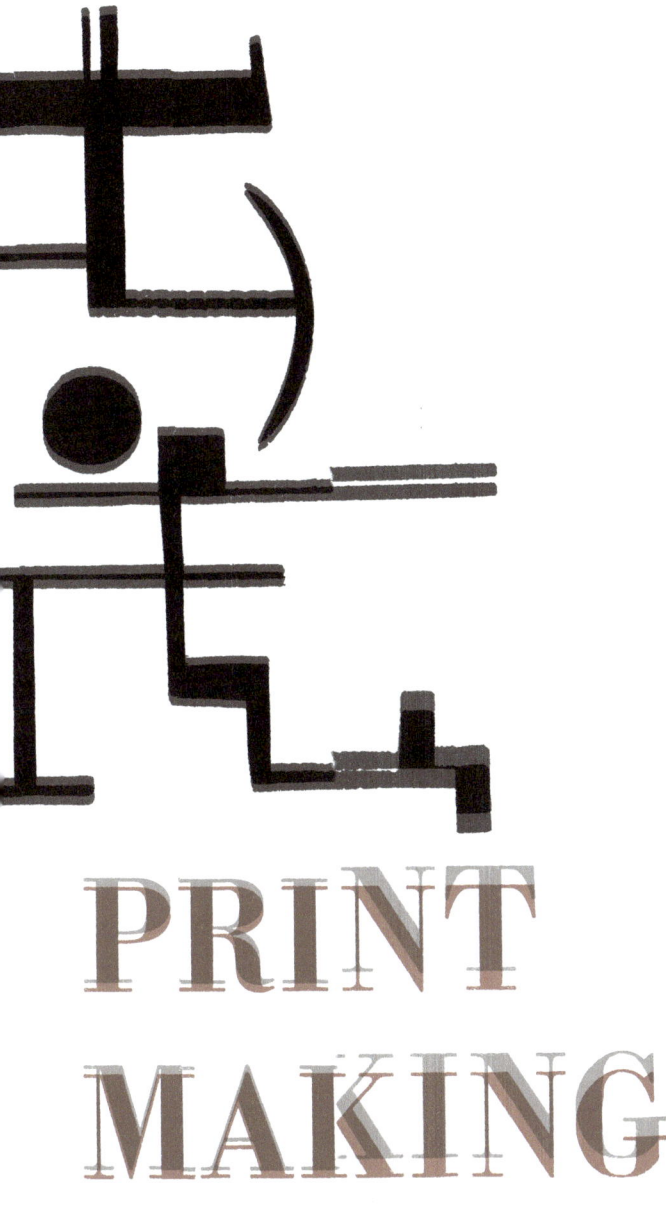

PRINT MAKING

THE UNIVERSITY OF VIRGINIA PRESS

Copyright, 1954, by Charles Smith, Manufactured in the United States of America.

Facsimile Edition
Published 2020
by Liber Apertus Press
Saratoga, California

ISBN 978-1-7342224-0-1

www.liberapertus.com
books@liberapertus.com

EXPERIMENTS IN RELIEF
PRINT MAKING

The purpose of this book is to suggest means and to show by example some experiments that may be used in expanding the range and scope of certain traditional methods used in making relief prints in color. There are deviations from the traditional, however, in that several of the methods described require but one engraved block for producing prints in any number of colors, while the traditional method requires a separate engraved block for each color used, and in another method the engraved block is not necessary at all for making prints in many colors. In the printing there is also a departure from the established methods. These experiments have been kept well within the limitations imposed by the materials used, and no attempt or effort has been made to make the final print resemble any other technique or medium.

The possibilities of obtaining interesting textures, patterns, and variations of color and values are limited only by the imagination and skill of the artist or student using them.

The methods described and illustrated represent much experimentation, and they are not offered as the final word in accomplishment. While no apology is made for the finished prints, it must be understood that from necessity they were printed on a mechanical power press and therefore, they lose much of the quality of hand-inked and hand-printed impressions.

PROCEDURE

It is essential that a drawing be made in color of the subject that is to be reproduced, and it should be the aim of the artist to follow this drawing as closely as possible in every stage. "Designing in the Material" can be done after much use of these methods, but for early experiments this procedure is not advised.

The general procedure is as follows: Make a drawing in color with shading texture and color clearly indicated. (Establish margins as shown on diagram in another part of this book.) Make a tracing of the drawing - if a key plate for direct printing is used as in *Still Life* the tracing must be reversed; if no key plate is to be used as in *Two Birds - Arrangement* the tracing need not be reversed but may be used right side up. In either case keep the margin as established on the original drawing. On all make-ready impressions for additional colors, textures, and patterns, this same margin must be kept to insure accurate registry of each impression as it is prepared for printing and later to insure registry as each color is printed.

The term "direct impression," as used here means that the block has been engraved as in *Still Life* and color transferred directly from the engraved block to the printing paper. The make-ready or indirect impression is different in that the pressure is applied to the reverse side of the paper causing the image to offset from a block to the printing paper. This impression is never as clear and sharp as the direct impressions. (See illustration.) Usually a combination of the two will produce softness and sharpness, although either may be used separately for certain desirable effects. *Arrangement* is an example of indirect impression.

Make-ready is a process used by printers for equalizing the pressure on printed impressions. The use of the process in making color prints as described here has the opposite purpose, although the means of accomplishing each is essentially the same. In print making, make-ready is used for obtaining light and dark values from a flat printing surface that normally produces only one value. The change of value is achieved by building up the printing surface for dark values and lowering the surface for light values. This is done by pasting, cutting, scraping or sanding chip board.

Printing is best accomplished by applying a thin uniform film of ink to the block by means of a brayer. When the printing is being done from make-ready impressions the ink is applied to the face of an uncut block either of wood or linoleum. The printing paper is then placed on the inked surface of the uncut block and the make-ready placed face down on the printing paper, in correct register. Pressure is then applied causing the image to offset to the paper in variations of values and textures as was planned in the drawing that is being reproduced. When printing from direct impressions, the brayer is used for applying ink to the raised or unengraved surface of the block as in the traditional manner of doing relief printing.

THE PLATES

In printing the plates the following order has been observed in each process. First the completed color print is shown. Following this a proof for each color is reproduced either from the direct impression or from a make-ready one. In no case is there more than two thicknesses of chip board used in the make-ready impressions for obtaining the darkest values. The sharp edges are easily distinguishable from the sanded ones. Similar effects in print making can be achieved by closely following these impressions.

STILL LIFE

A key block method, printed from four make-ready impressions and one direct impression.

A drawing was made in color of the subject. From this drawing an outline was traced. This in turn was reversed and transferred to a linoleum block. The block was cut with a knife. This black block was used as a key for color separation and registration. Impressions from the key block were made on chip board, one for each color used. Dark values were built up and the lighter ones were lowered by cutting or sanding the chip board. This print required an additional uncut linoleum block the same size as the cut key block to be used as a background for the chip board impressions. The printing was done in the following order; the gray impression was printed first, the yellow second, the blue third, the green fourth, and the black last.

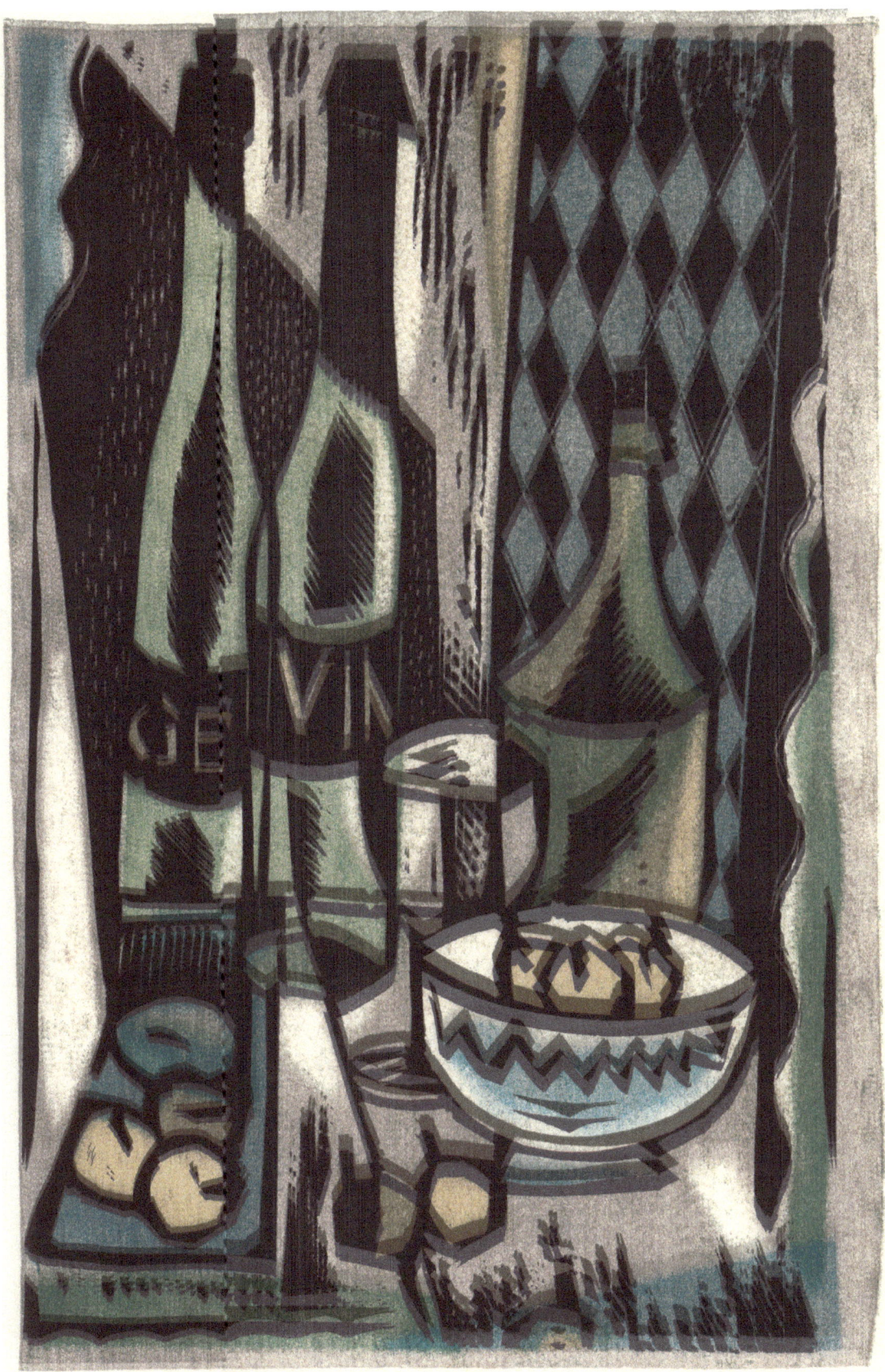

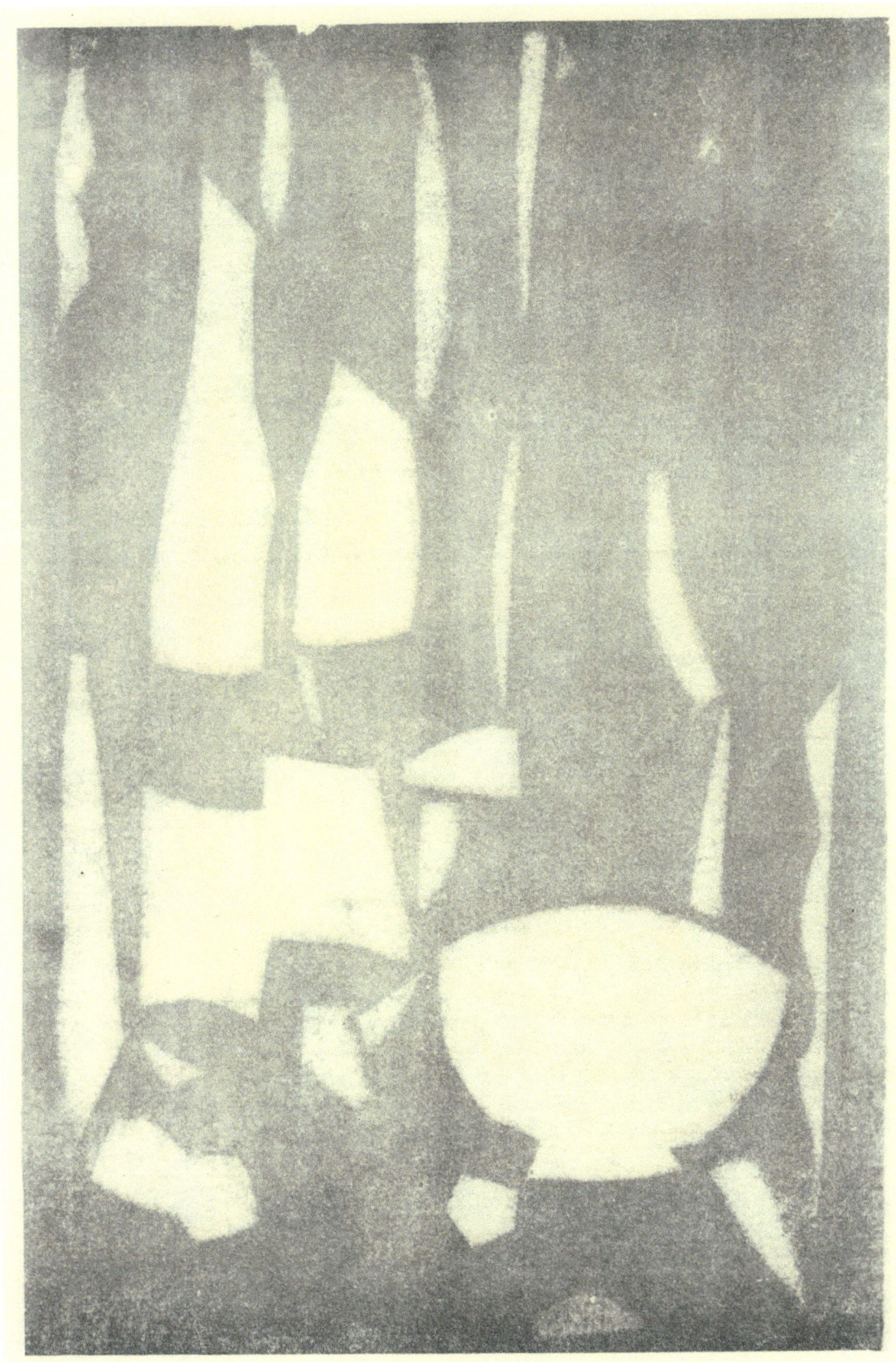

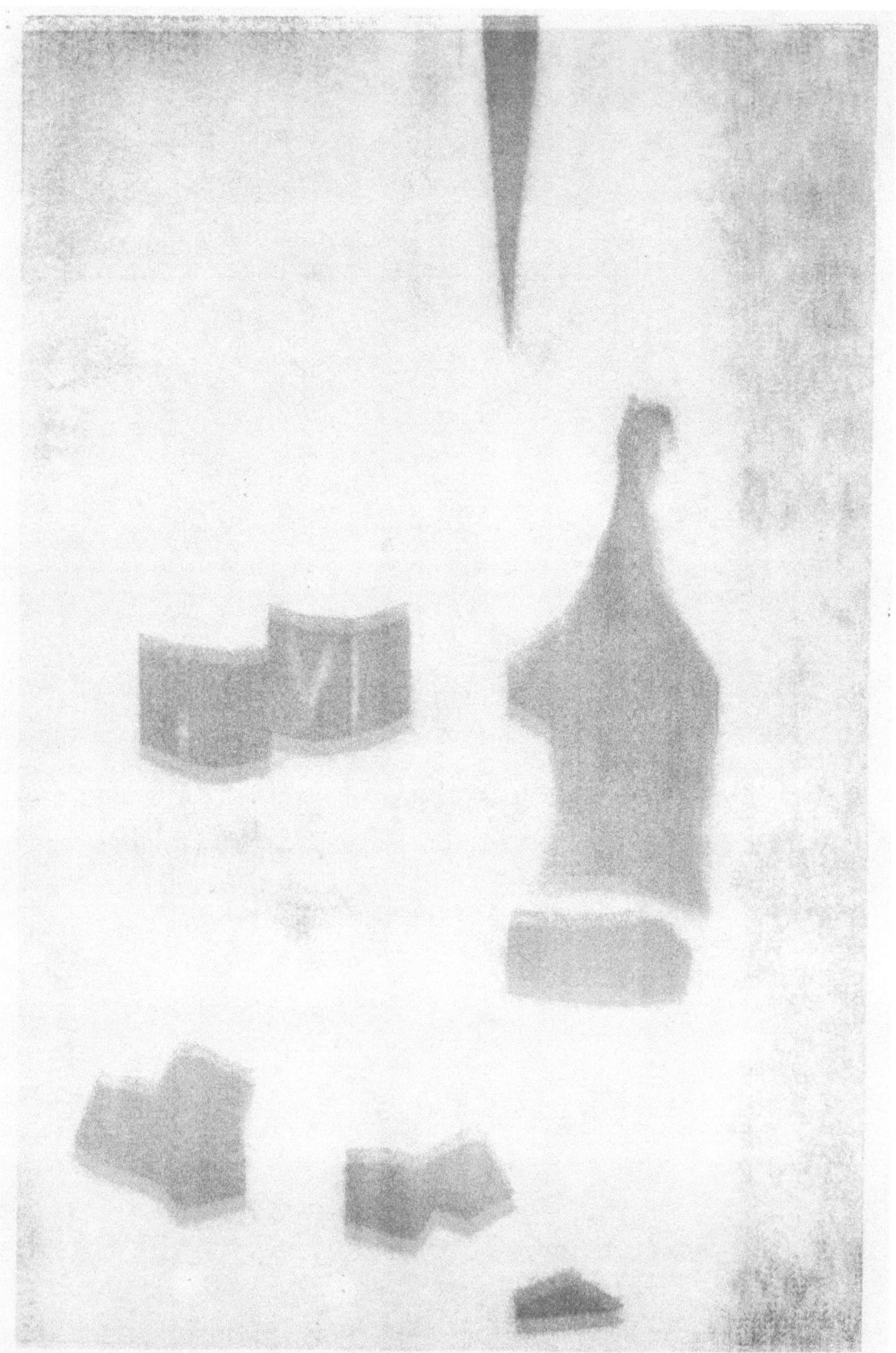

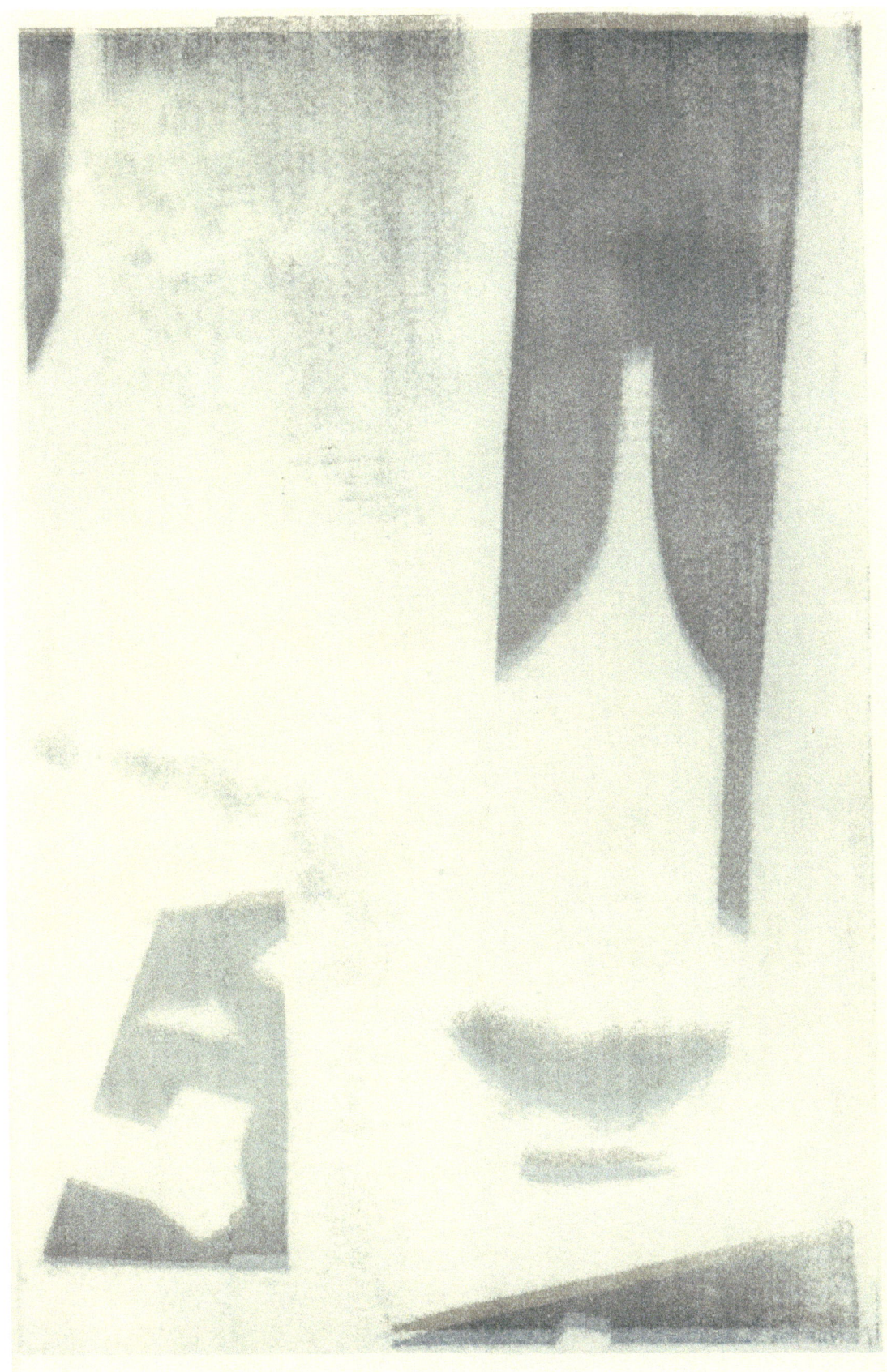

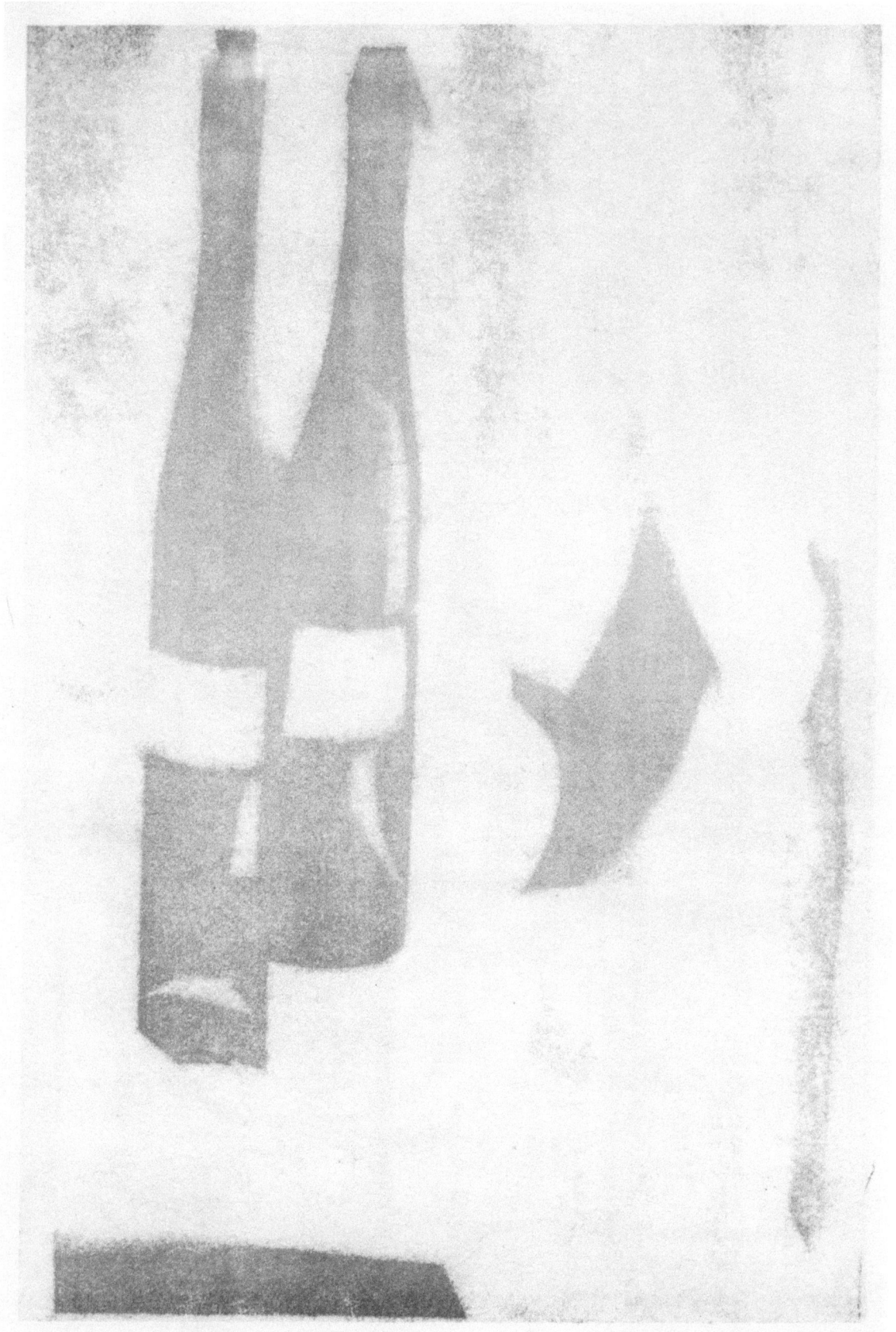

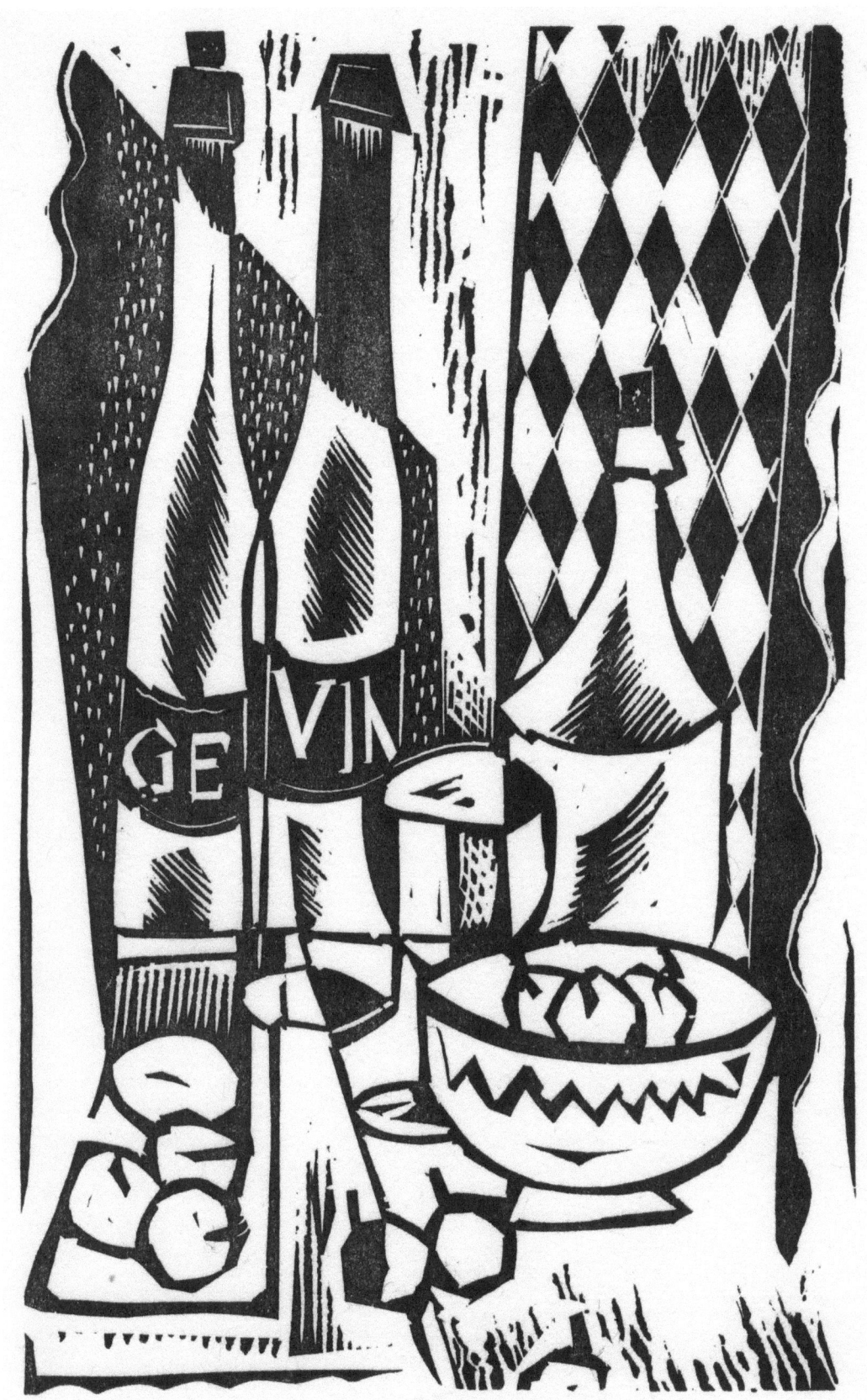

DARK ACCENTS

A pre-cut method printed from four direct impressions.

A drawing was made in color of the subject. From this drawing a tracing was made in outline, on heavy tracing paper. Four pieces of plywood were used and the tracing transferred in reverse and in register to each piece. The same tracing was then used for the separation of colors and shapes. All parts of the print that were to be light tan were traced in reverse on a piece of linoleum and cut out. They were then glued to the plywood tracing, each in its proper place. This procedure was followed for each color used. The colors were printed in the following order: light tan, dark tan, medium red, and black. The outline plate, following the black proofs of the print, was used as a guide in gluing the linoleum shapes to the plywood blocks and also as a guide to cutting the shapes in the linoleum for the various colors.

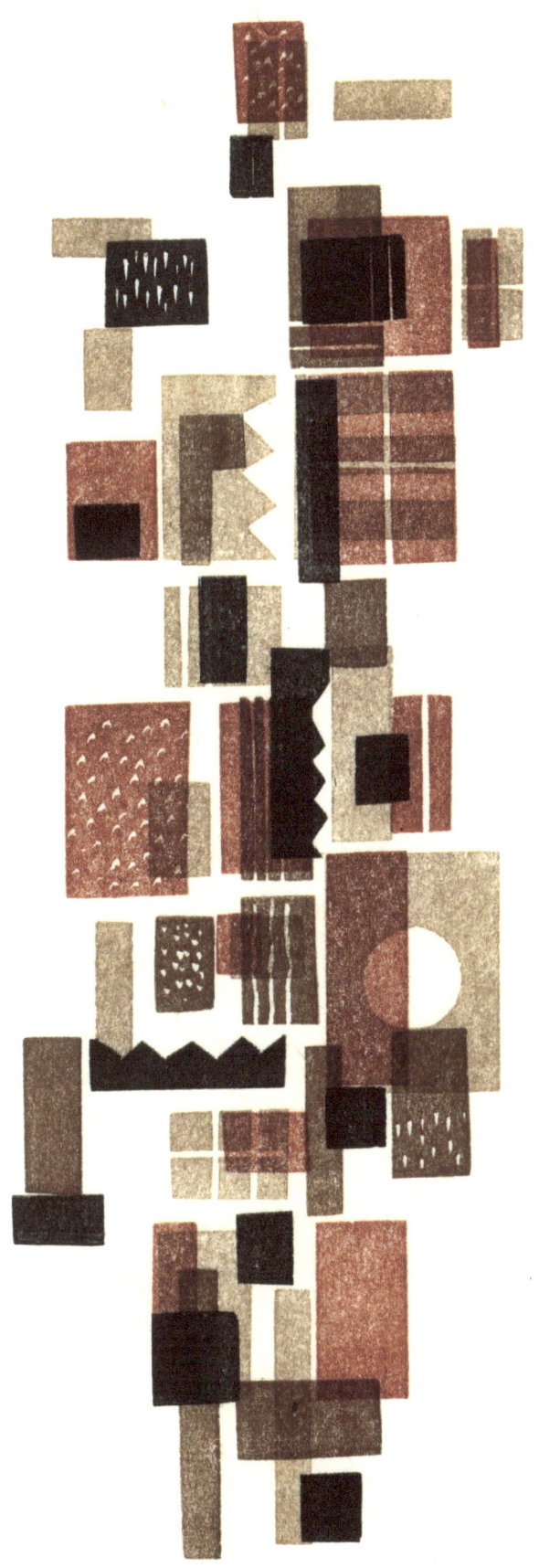

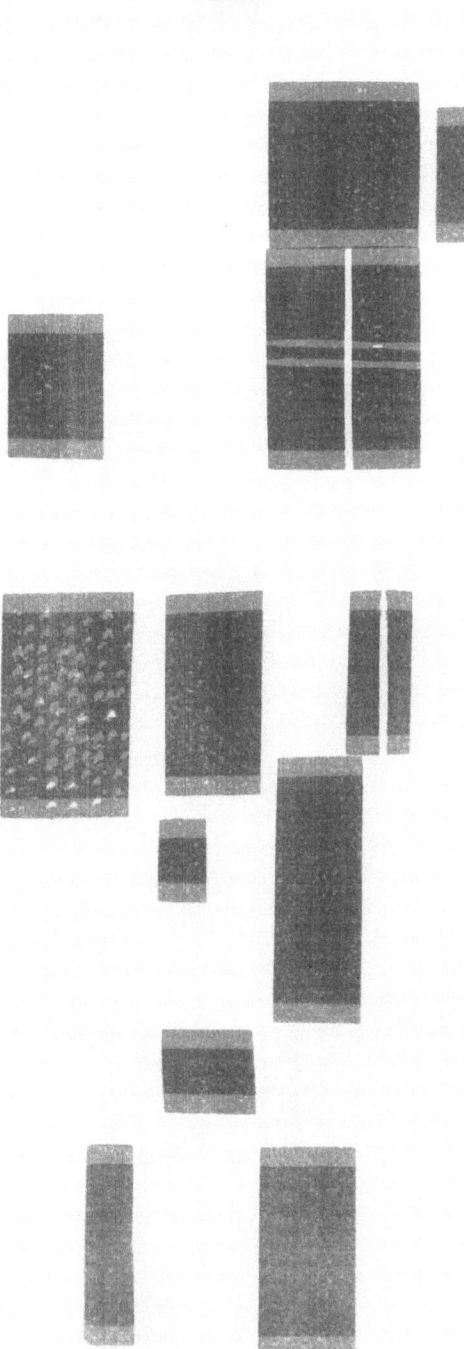

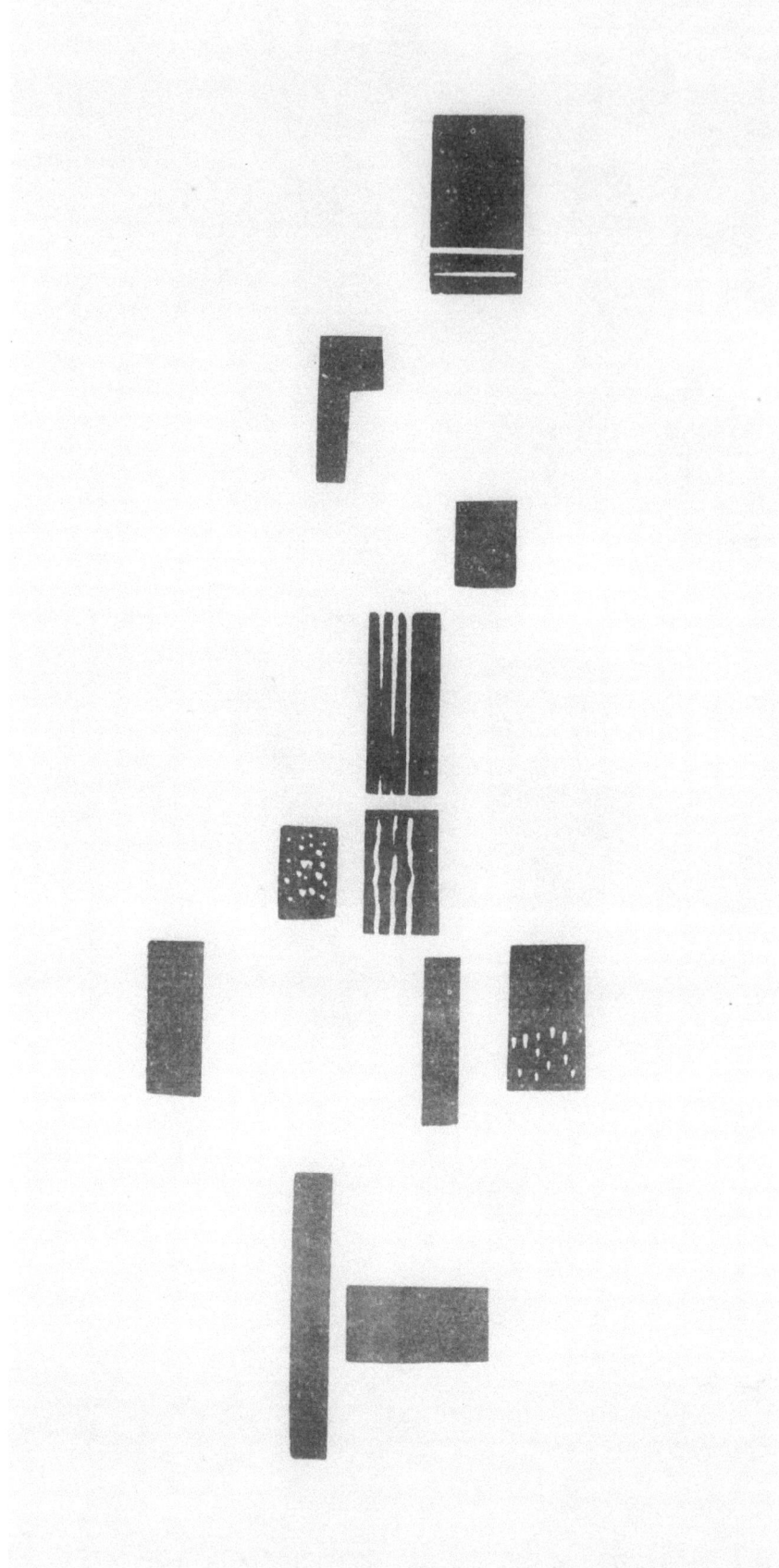

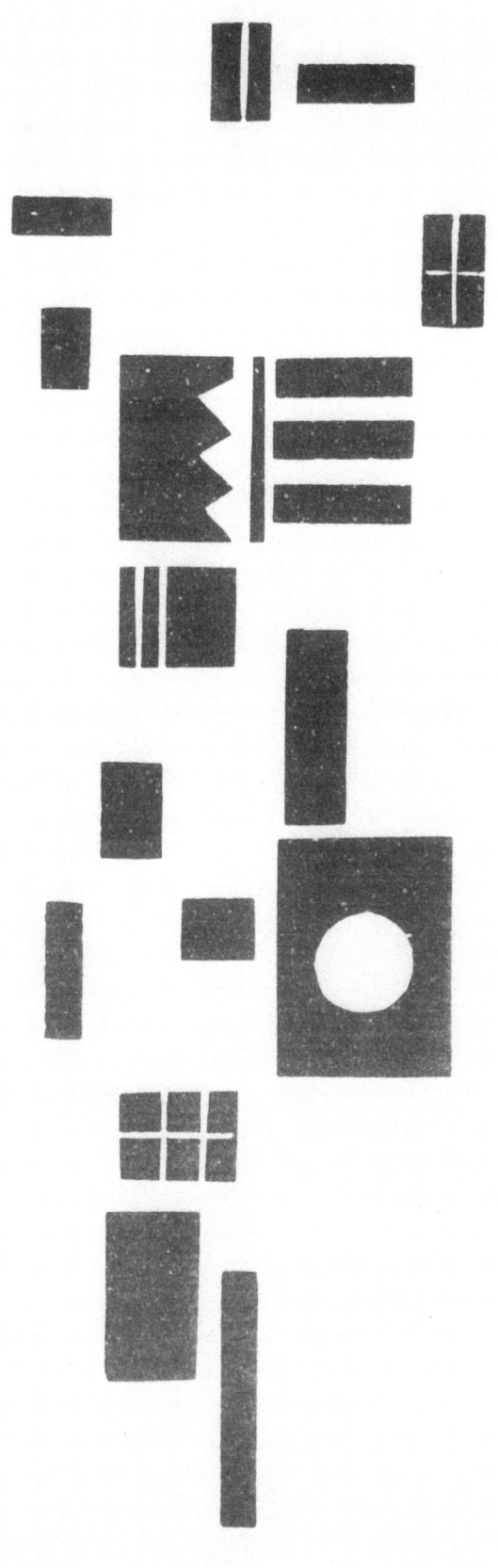

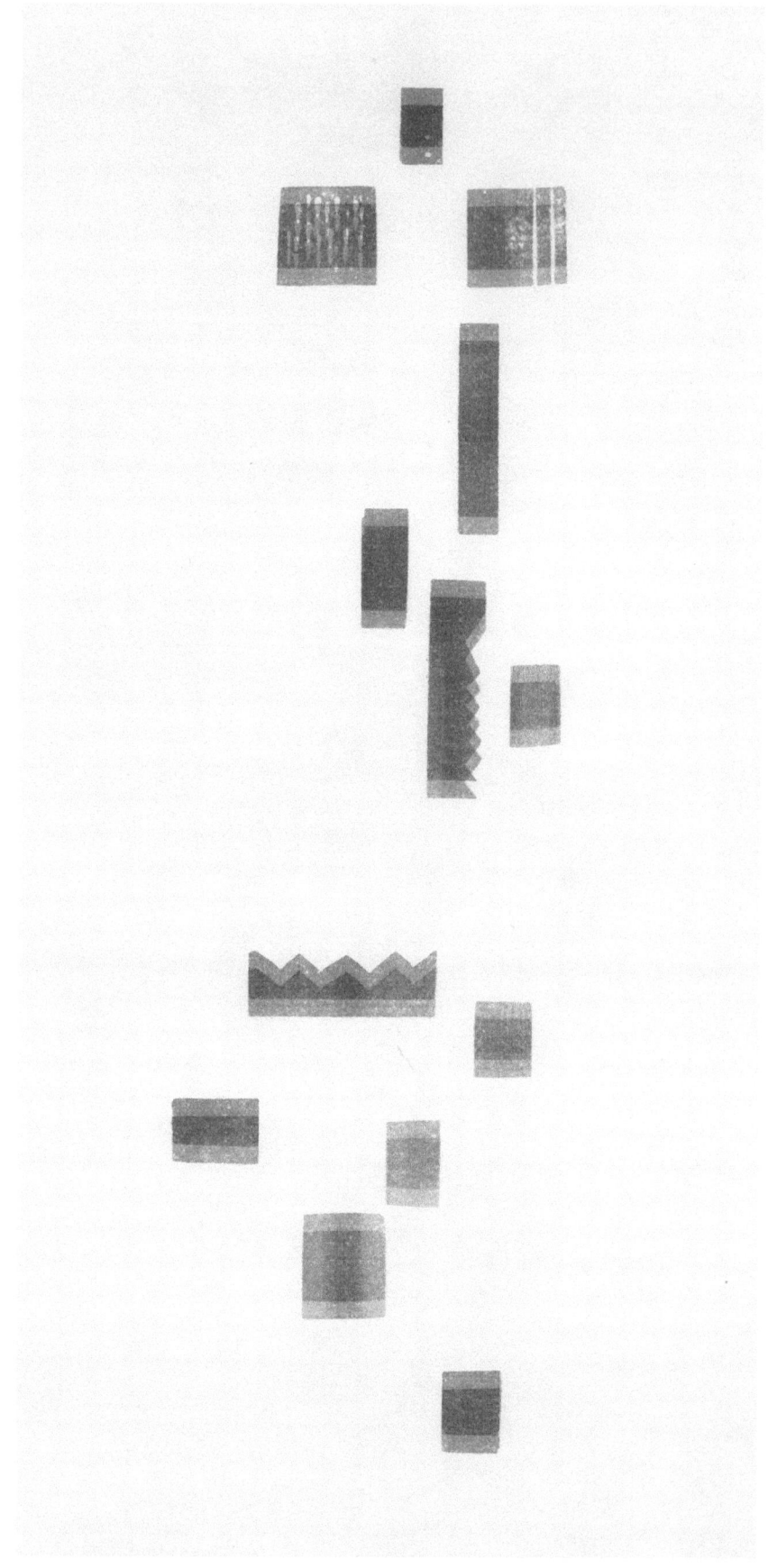

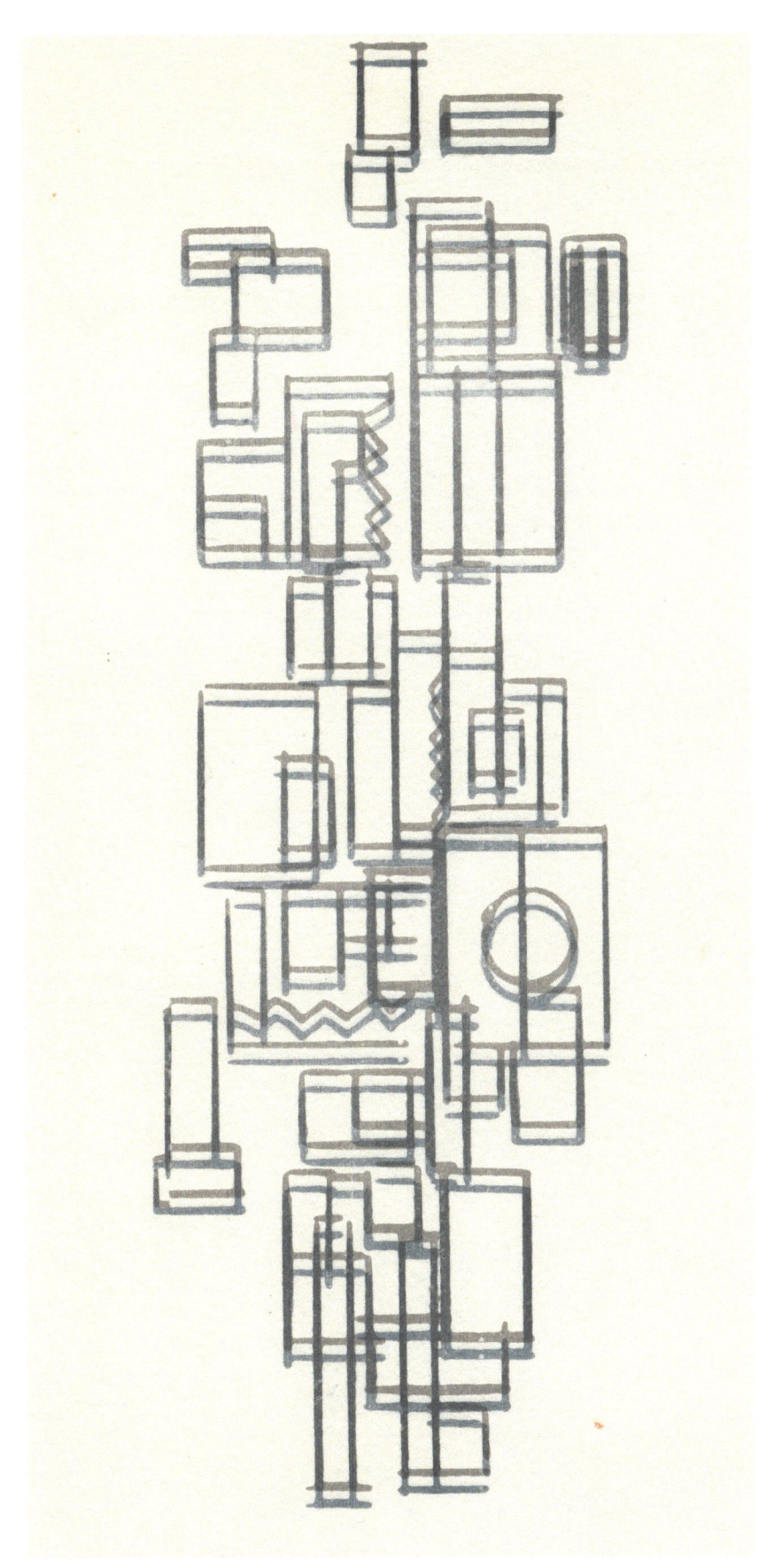

ARRANGEMENT

A collage method printed from four make-ready impressions.

A drawing was made in color of the subject. From this drawing a tracing was made on heavy tracing paper. Four pieces of chip board were used, these being of the same dimension and having the same margins as the drawing. The tracing was transferred by use of carbon paper to the chip boards, these four tracings were used for pasting up the make-ready. The next step was to trace on other pieces of chip board all red areas of the drawing; these were in turn cut out and pasted on to the outline in the proper places. This operation was followed for each color used. The order of printing was as follows. The buff with canvas background; the red shapes and the green; and, finally, the black with pasted-on brass ring and piece of string. These make-ready color impressions can easily be understood from the four black and white illustrations following the completed print.
The line tracing shown on the last page of this section was used as a guide for color separation and for pasting of chip board make-ready, in the correct positions.

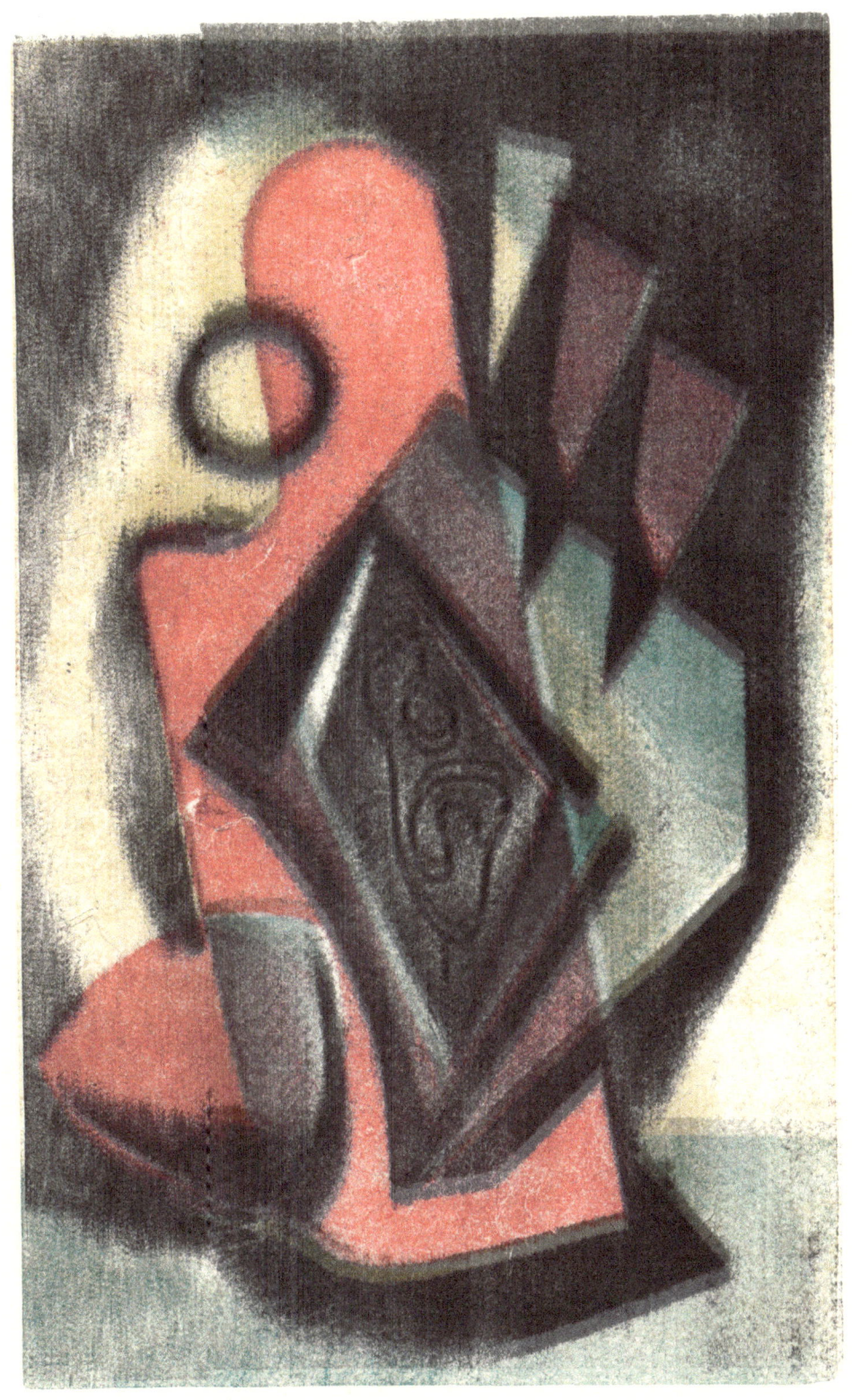

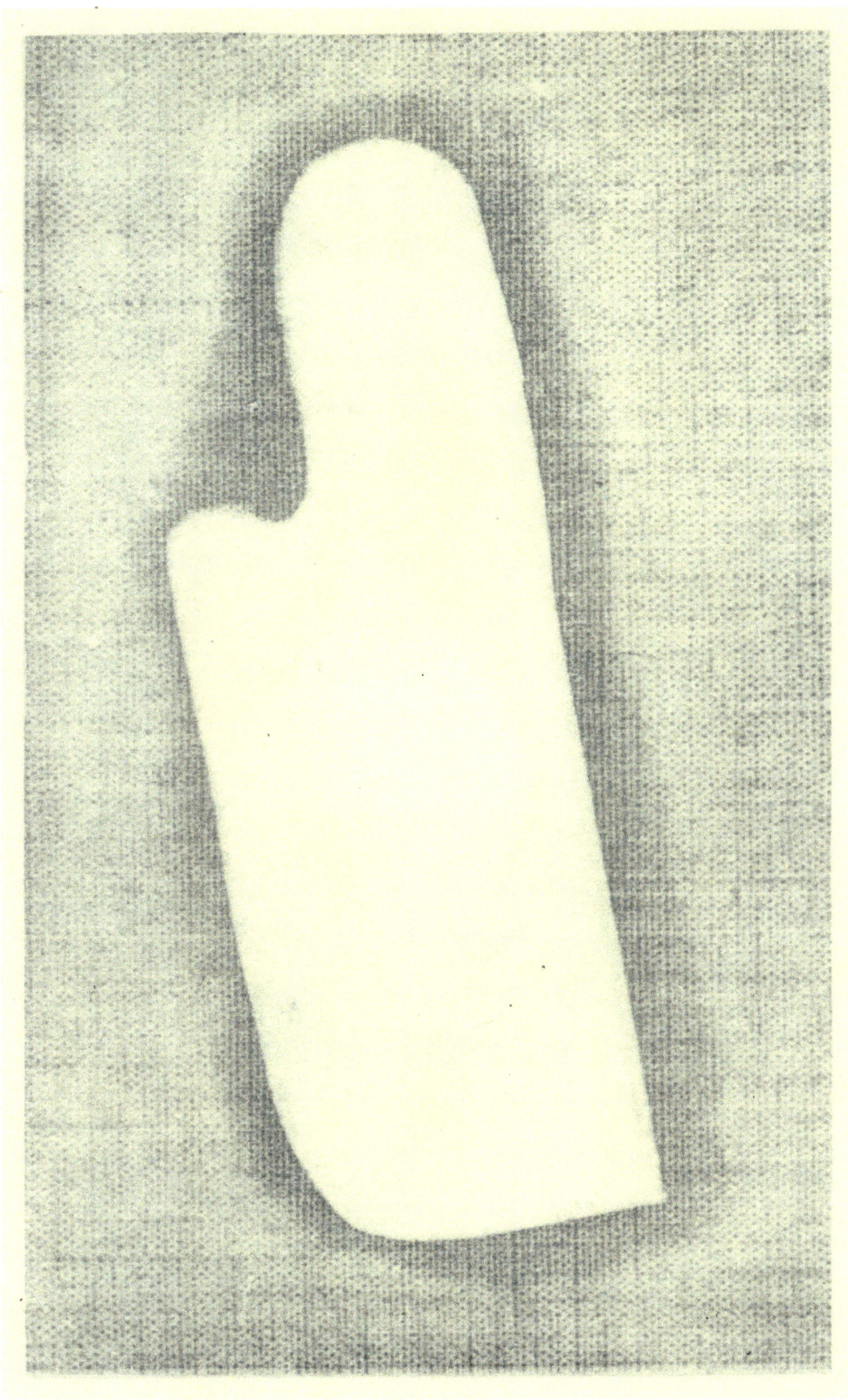

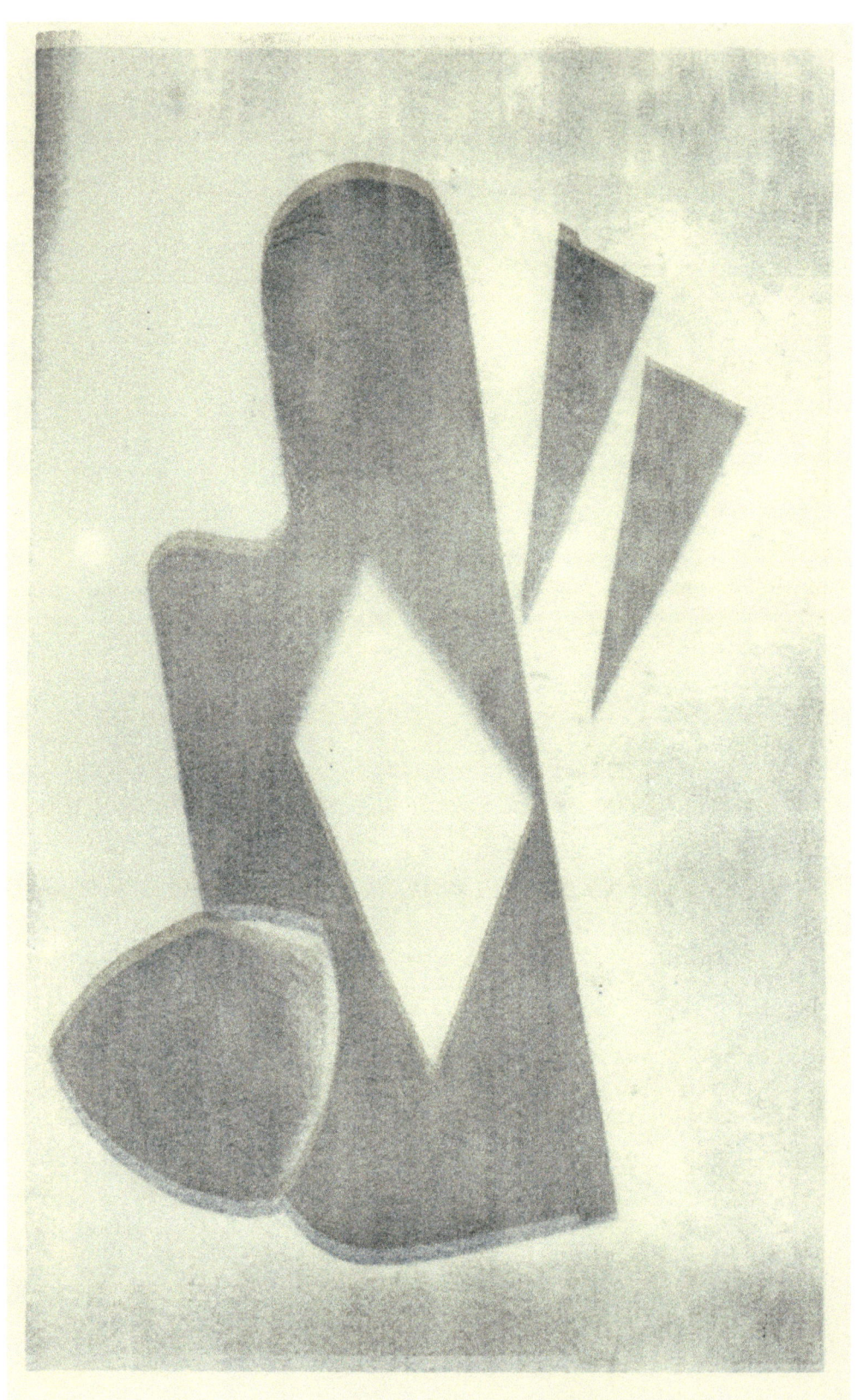

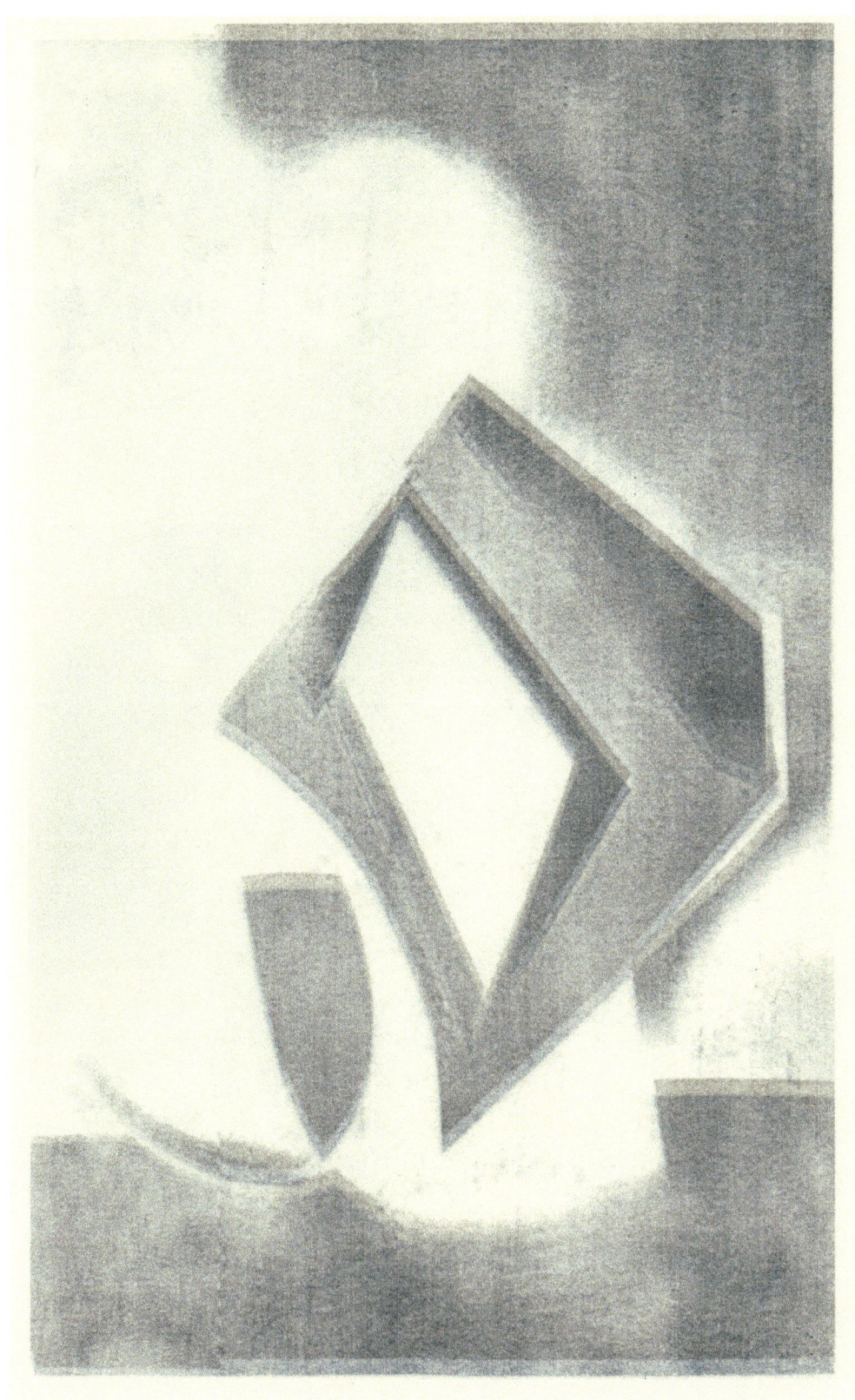

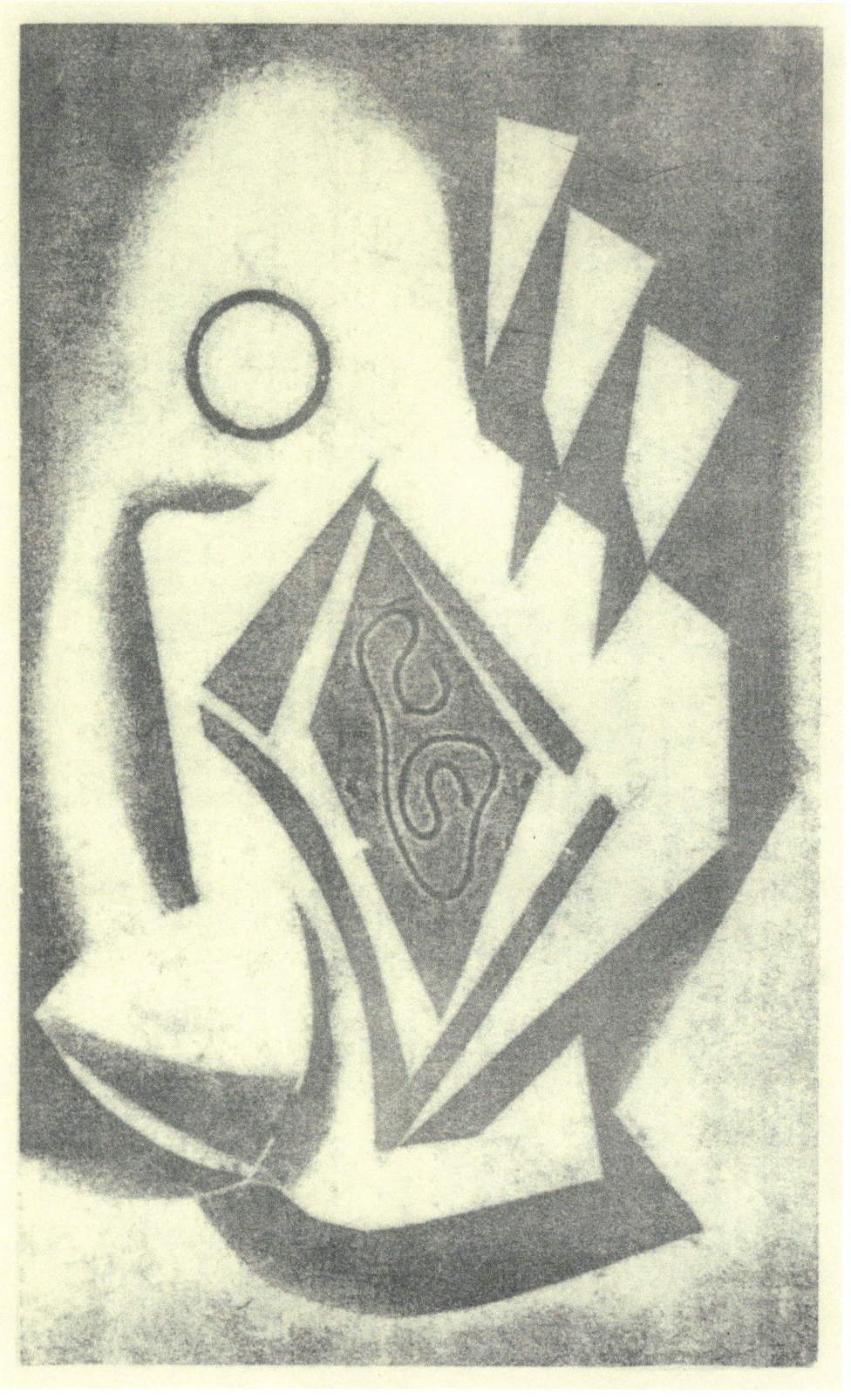

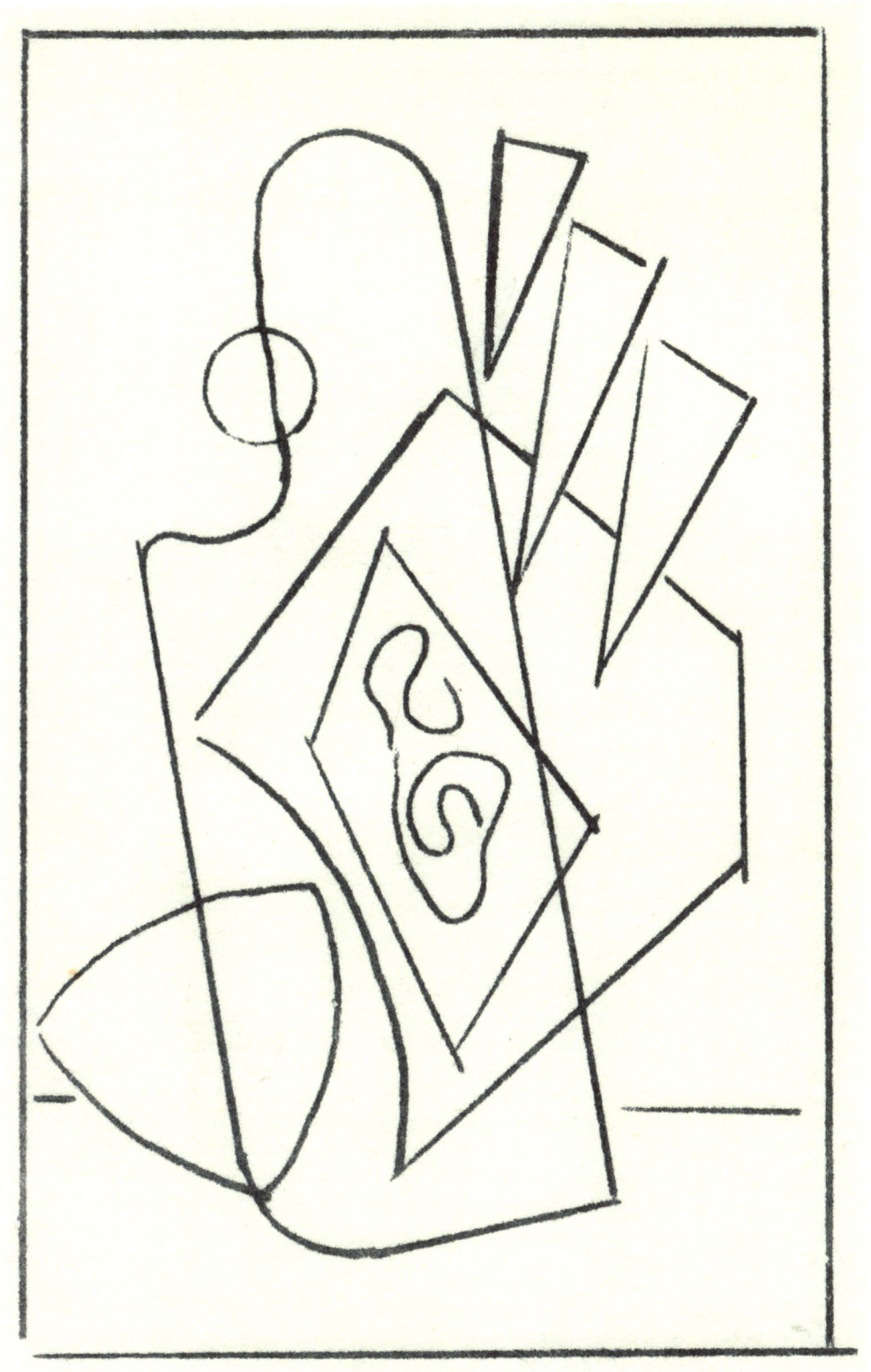

COMPOSITION

A subtractive method from four direct impressions made from the same block.

A drawing was made in color of the subject. From this drawing a tracing was made of one color only. This tracing was reversed and transferred to the linoleum block and cut with a knife and a gouge. Then it was printed in a grayish tint. The block was removed from the press and the next color traced on the block and cut. It was then printed in a grayish green color. The block was removed from the press and the darkish green traced and cut. This was then printed - and lastly, the block was once more removed from the press and the final color, dark green, traced and cut and printed. The last plate shown in this section represents the drawing in color of the subject reproduced.

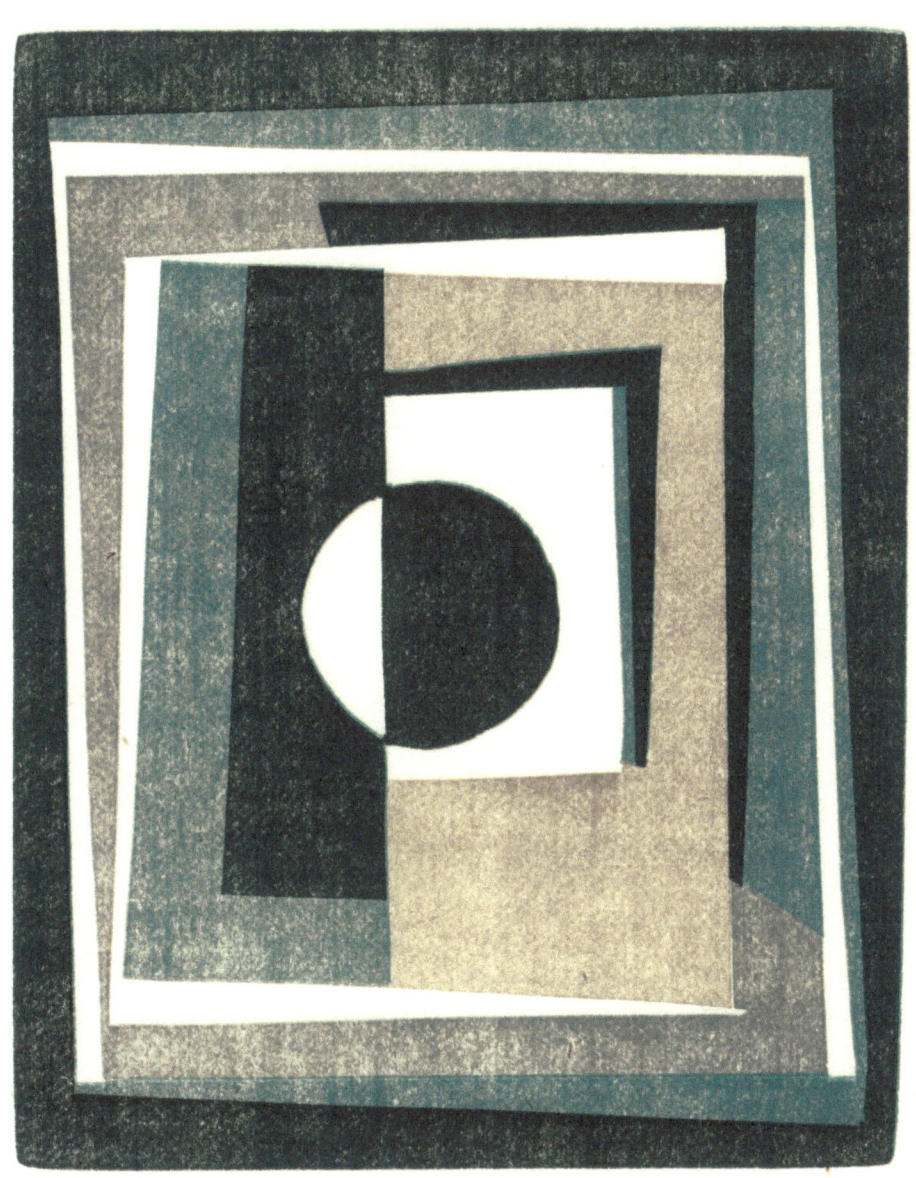

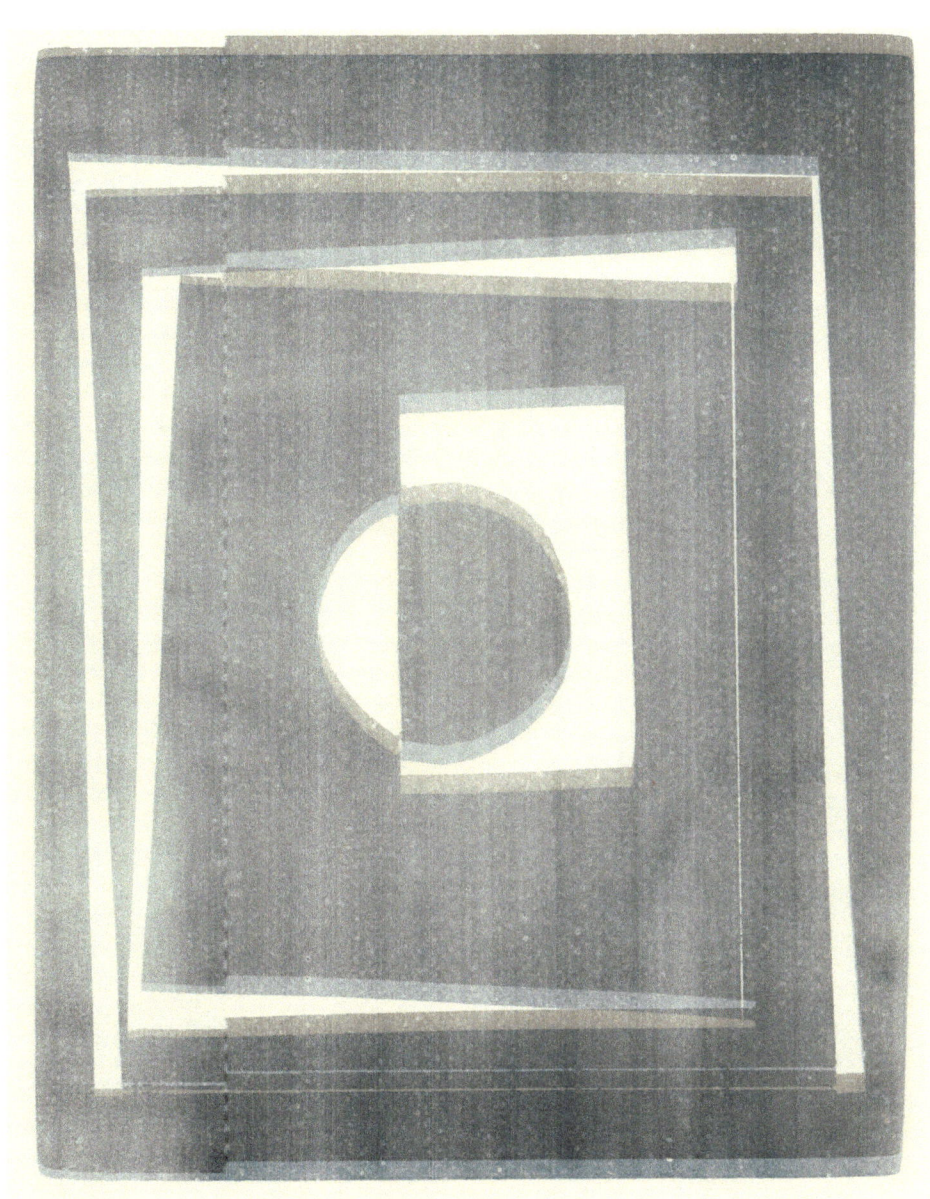

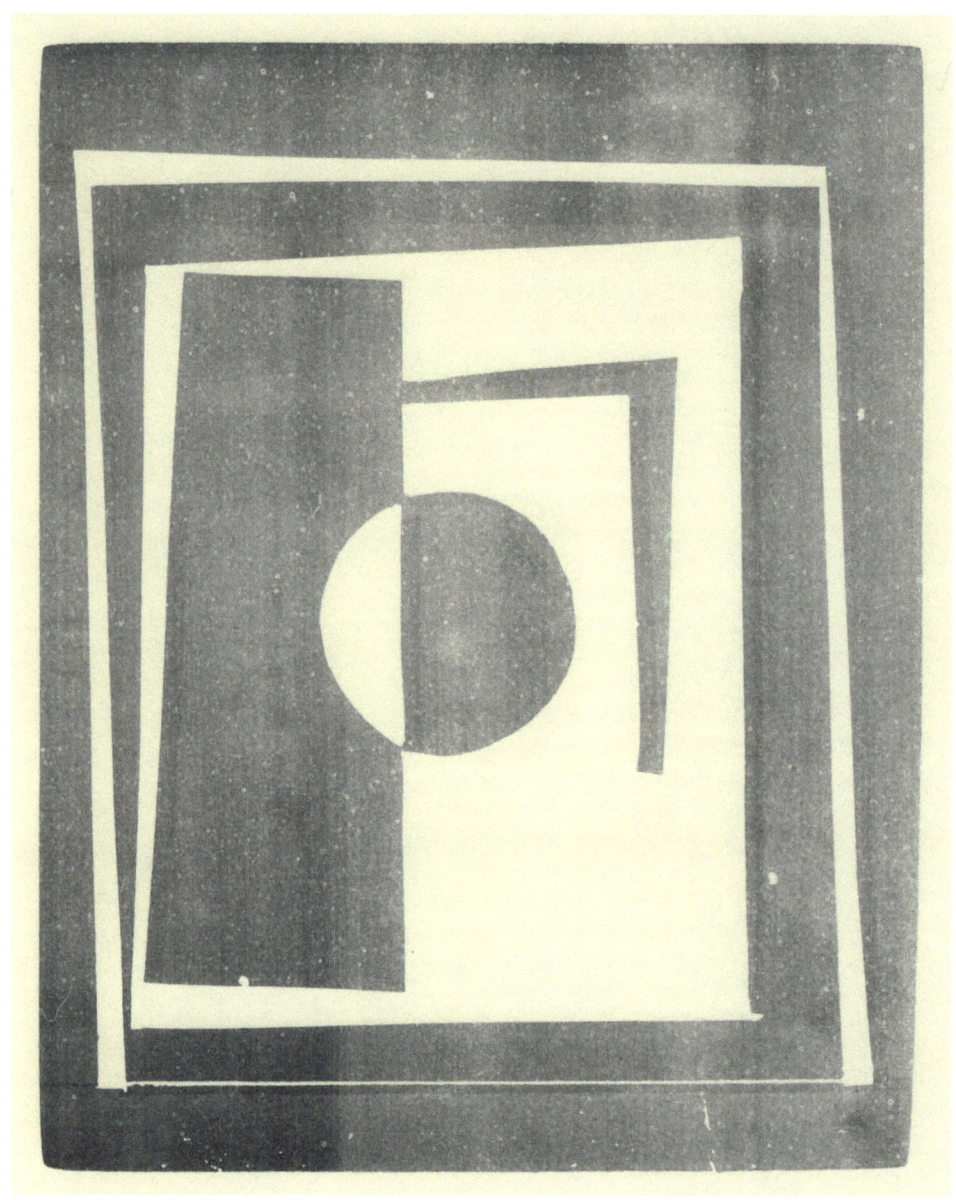

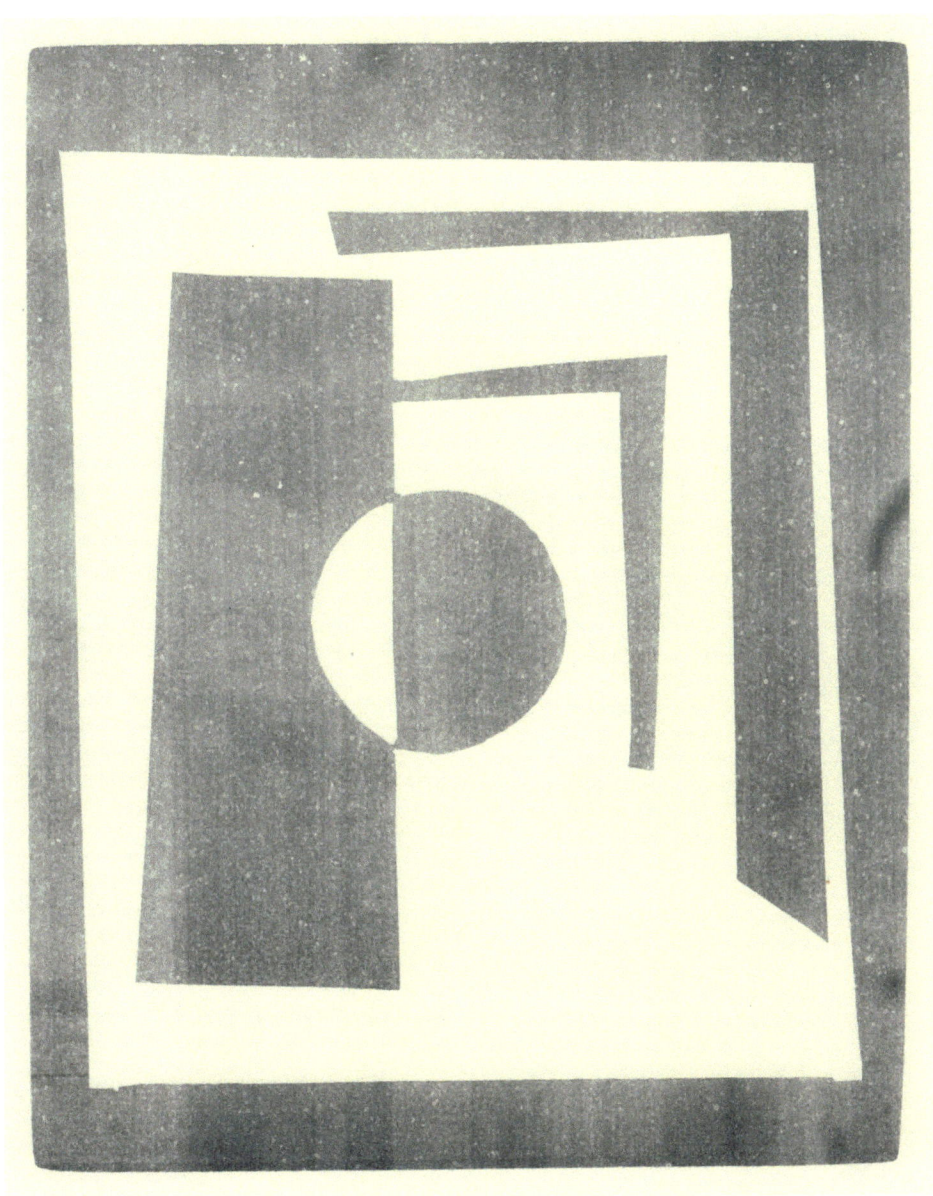

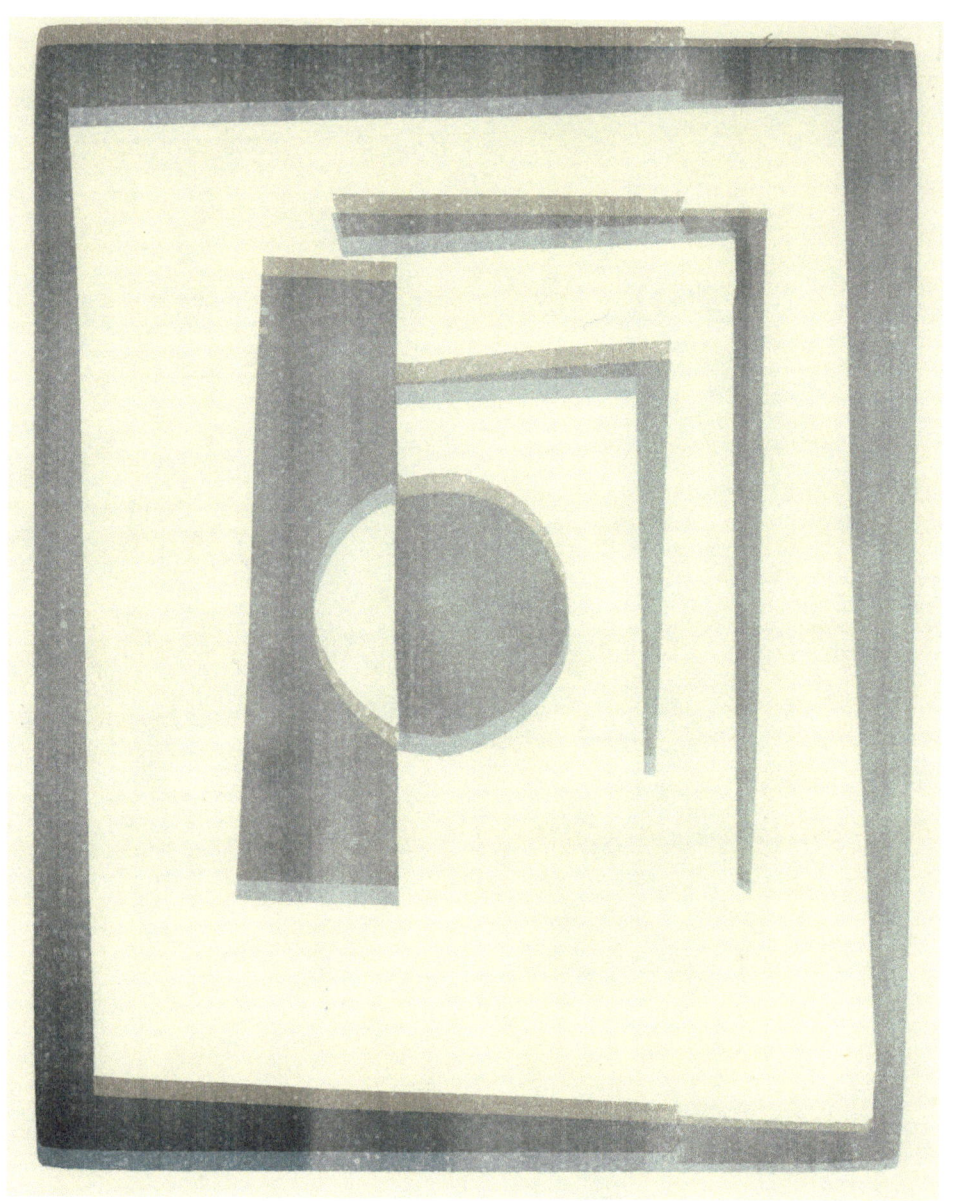

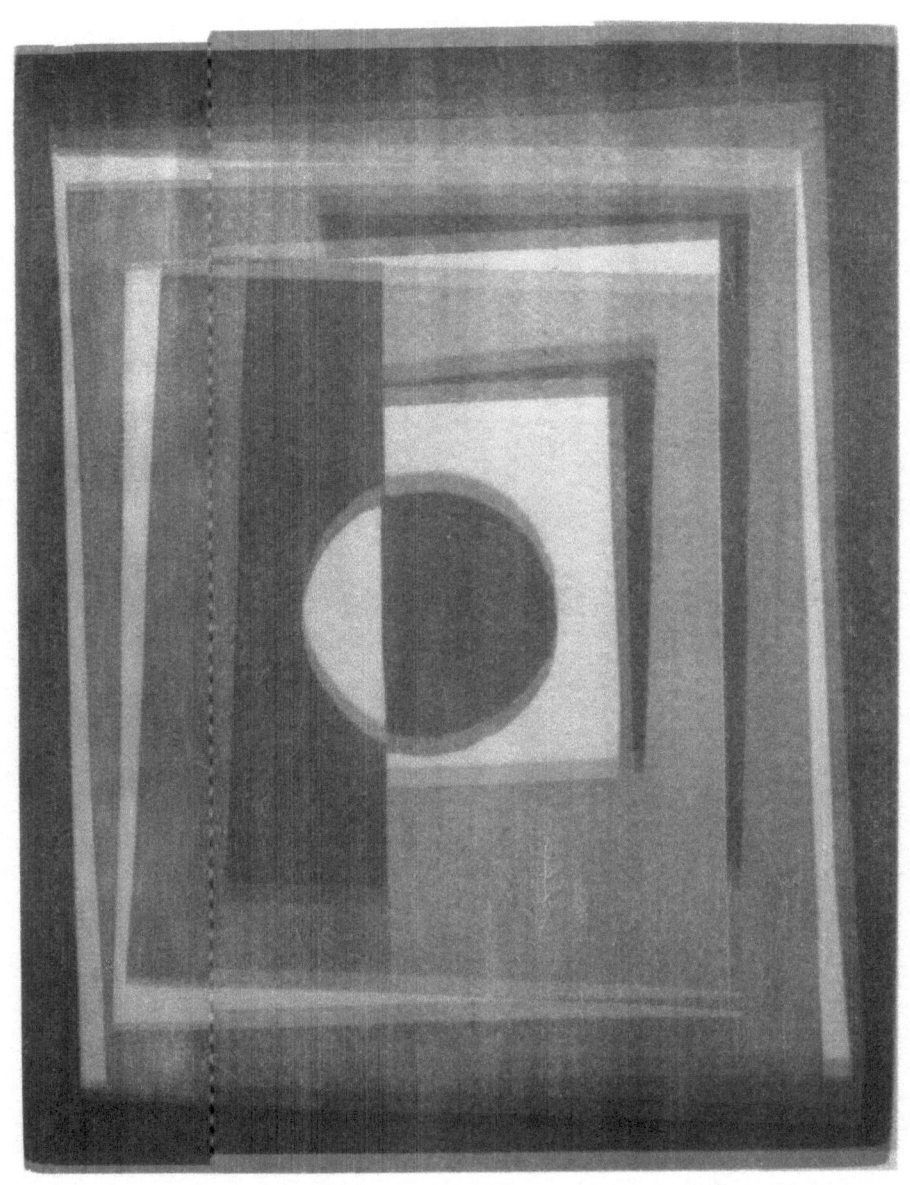

TWO BIRDS

A white line method, printed from four make-ready impressions and one direct impression.

A drawing was made in color of the subject. From this drawing an outline was traced. This in turn was reversed and transferred to a linoleum block. The block was engraved in a thin white line, with a standard wood engraving tool. This white line block was used as a key for color separation and registration. Impressions from this key block were made on chip board, one for each color used. The dark values were built up and the light ones cut out or lowered by sanding or scraping. The pages following the completed print show each step of the make-ready, and were printed in the following order; brown, yellow, blue, and gray, the last impression being black which was a direct impression from a block. In this particular print the white line key plate shown on the make-ready plates was not used, except for demonstration purposes. The key plate that was used was done with a dry point tool in a lighter line which makes it far less evident in the completed print.

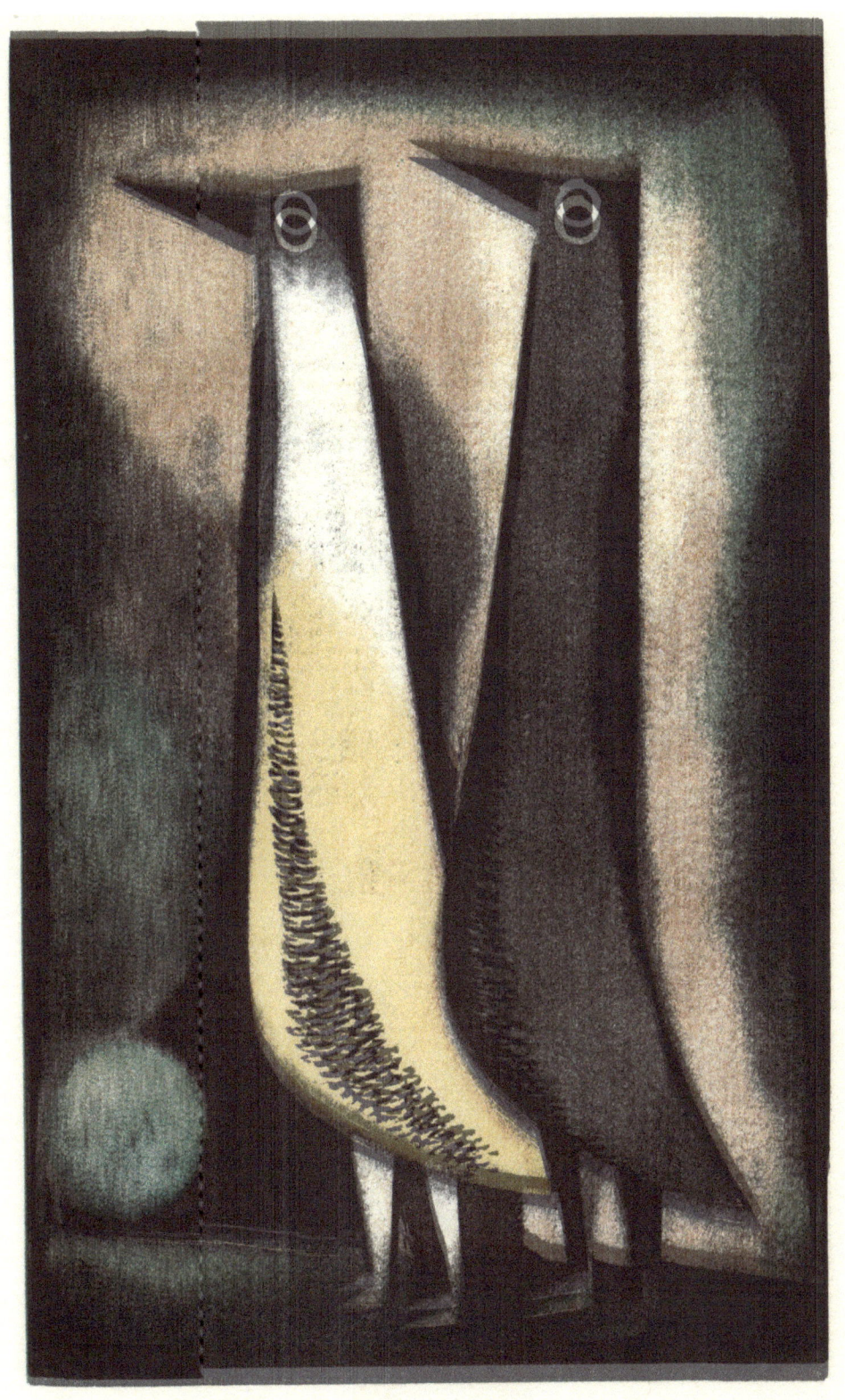

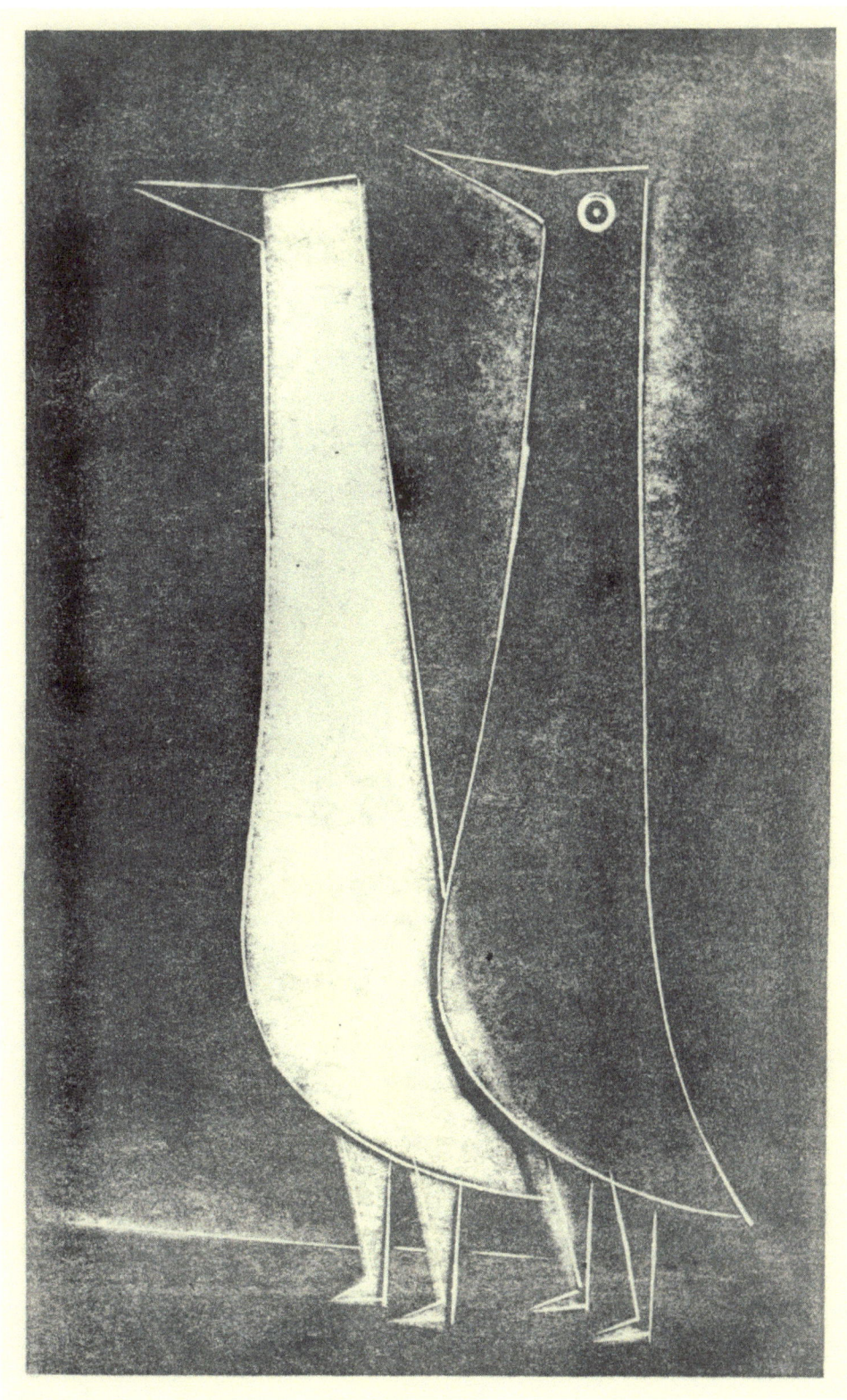

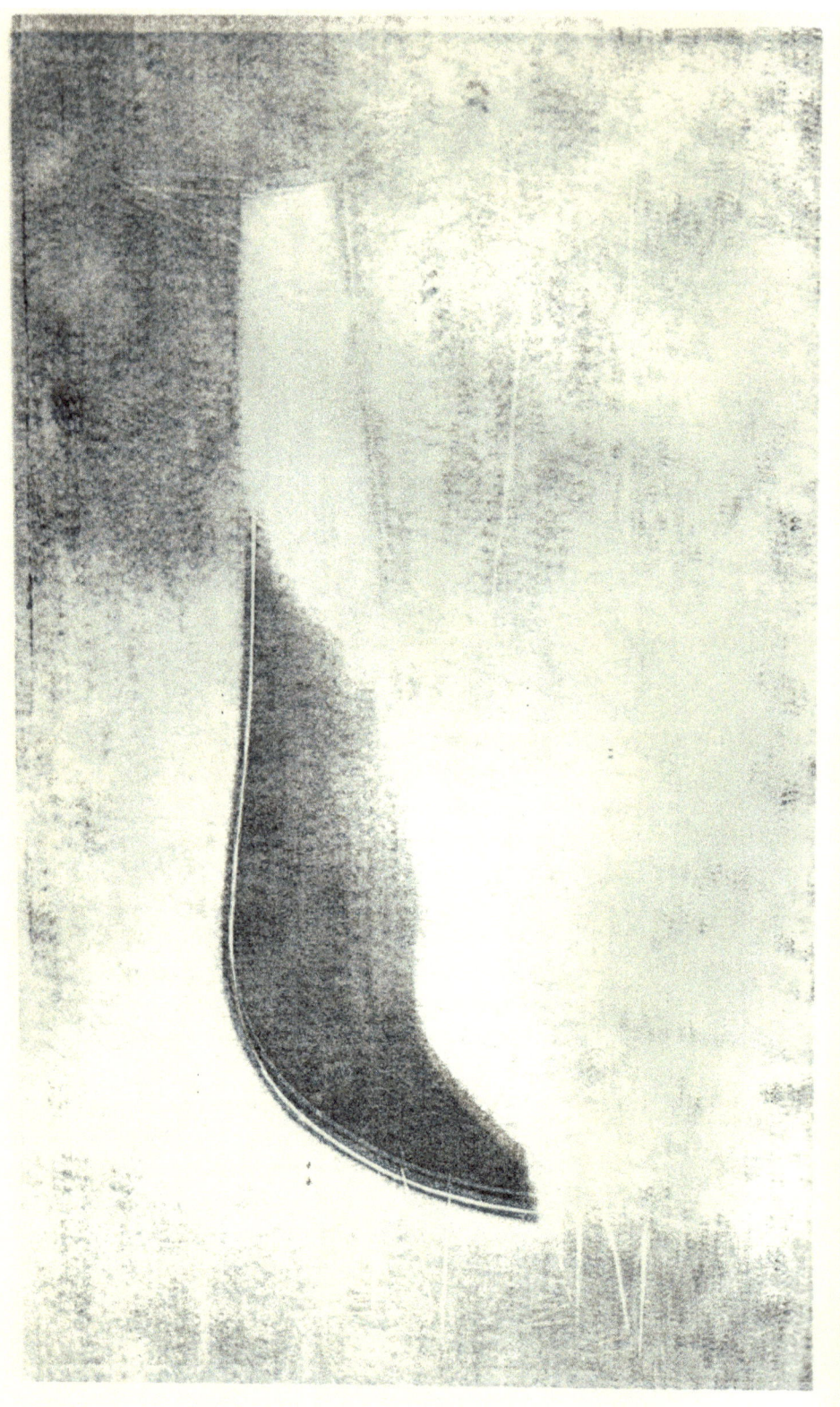

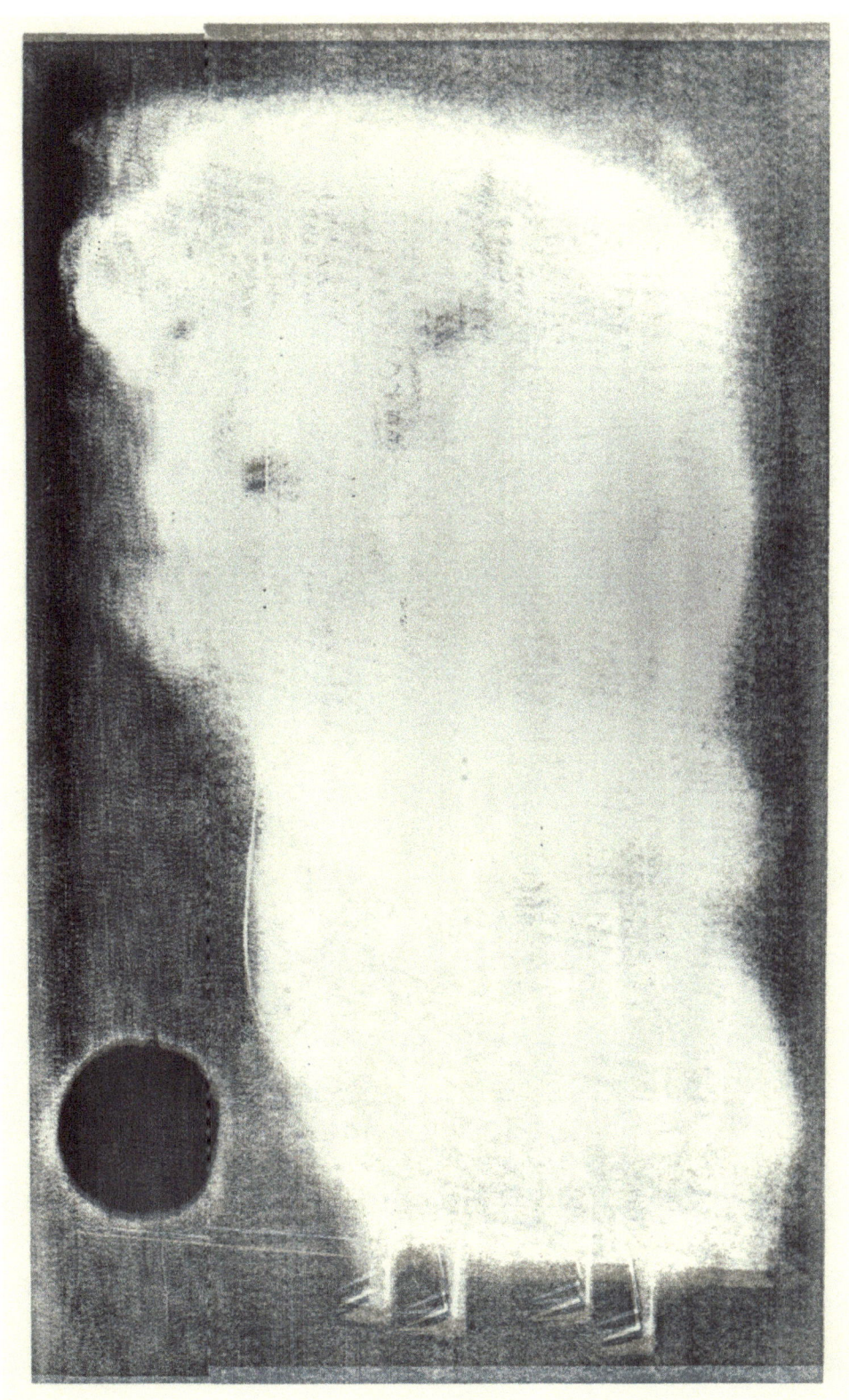

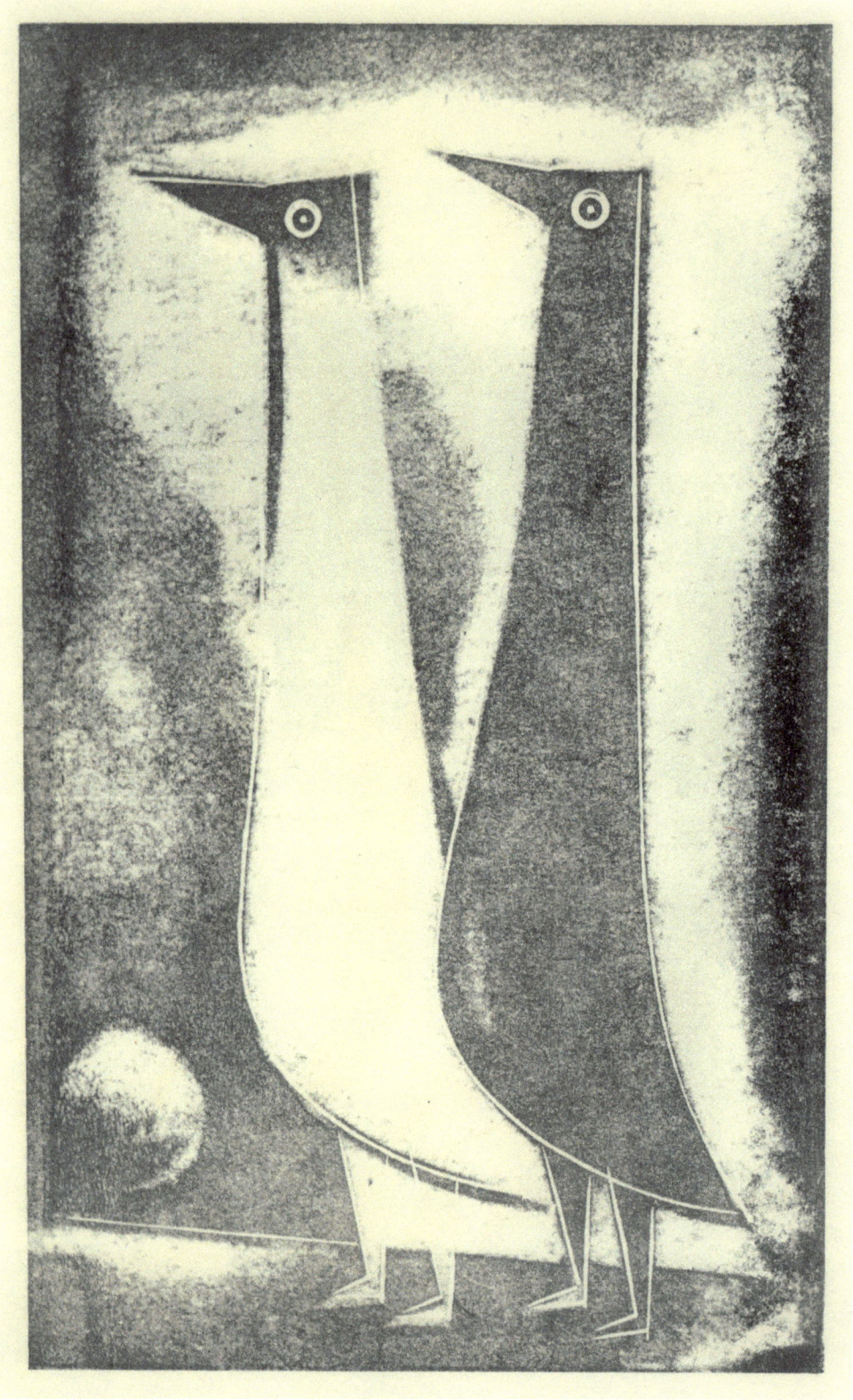

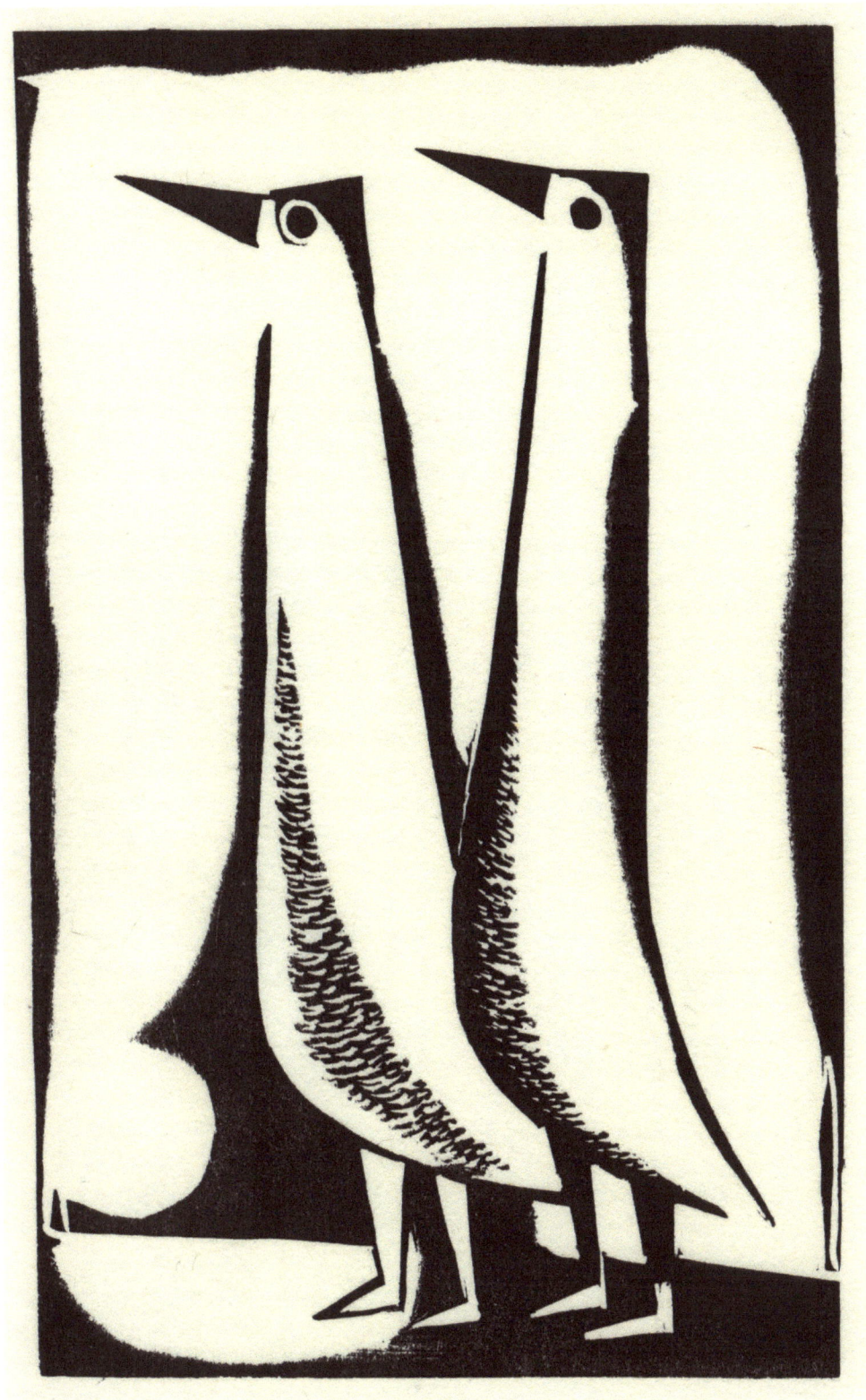

TWO DISCS

A movable shape method, printed from one make-ready impression and three direct impressions.

A drawing was made in color of the subject. The shapes used were traced on a piece of end maple, the kind used for engravings. These shapes were then sawed out on a jig or band saw. Tracings were made of the drawing and transferred to pieces of cardboard, one for each color used. The shapes were then glued to the cardboard in the proper places as was shown on the original drawing, all in correct register. The three colors were proofed and from this proof the make-ready impression was made on chip board. This is shown in the first plate following the completed color print. This print was done in two colors and the order of printing is shown in the black and white illustrations following the completed print. The last black and white illustration in this section shows one of the printing plates with the sawed out shapes glued to the cardboard guide.

This method is very flexible as a collection of shapes can be made and used in various combinations for different prints. The shape is removed from the cardboard and the glued-down side cleaned off, and is ready to be used again.

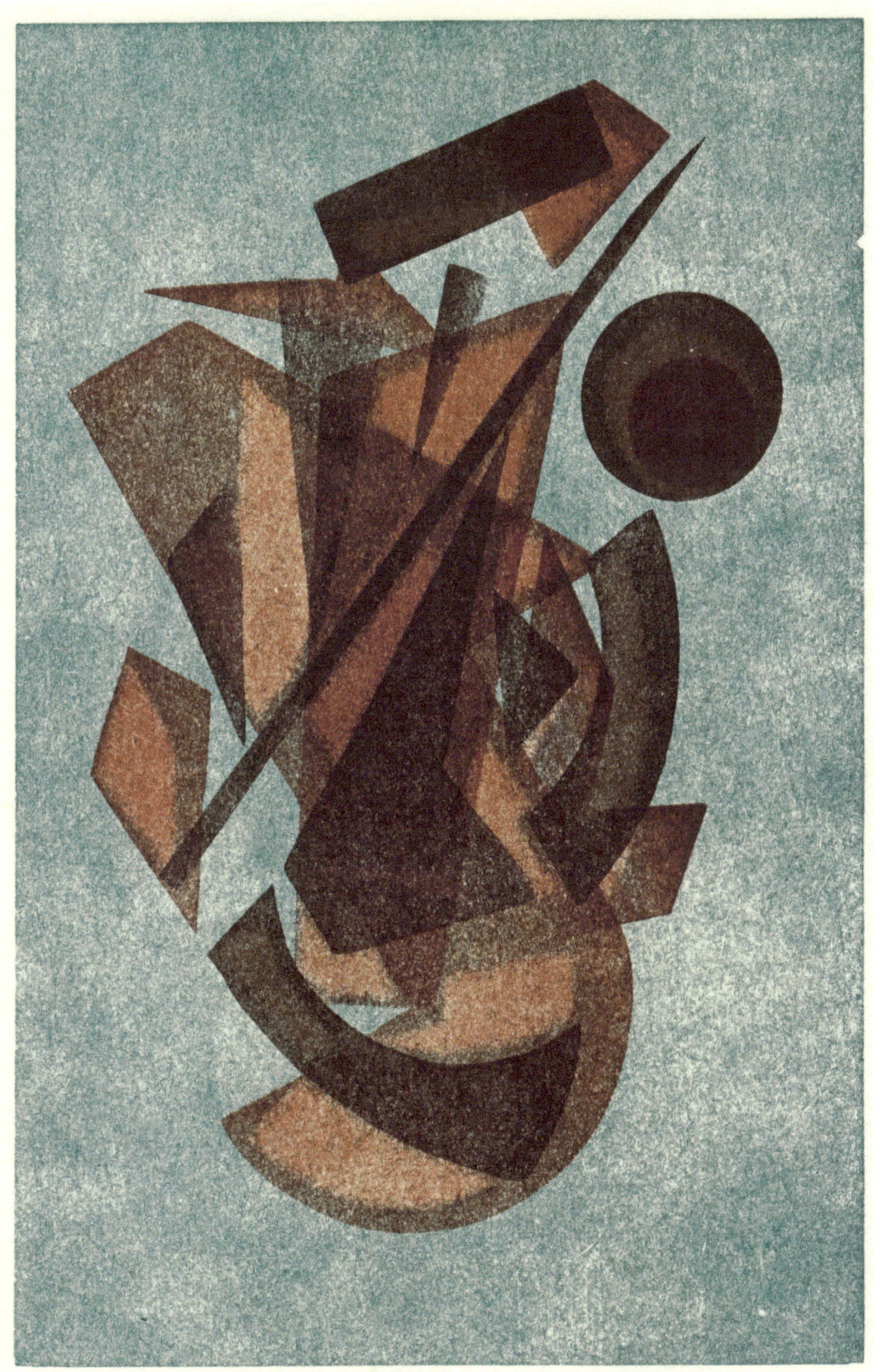

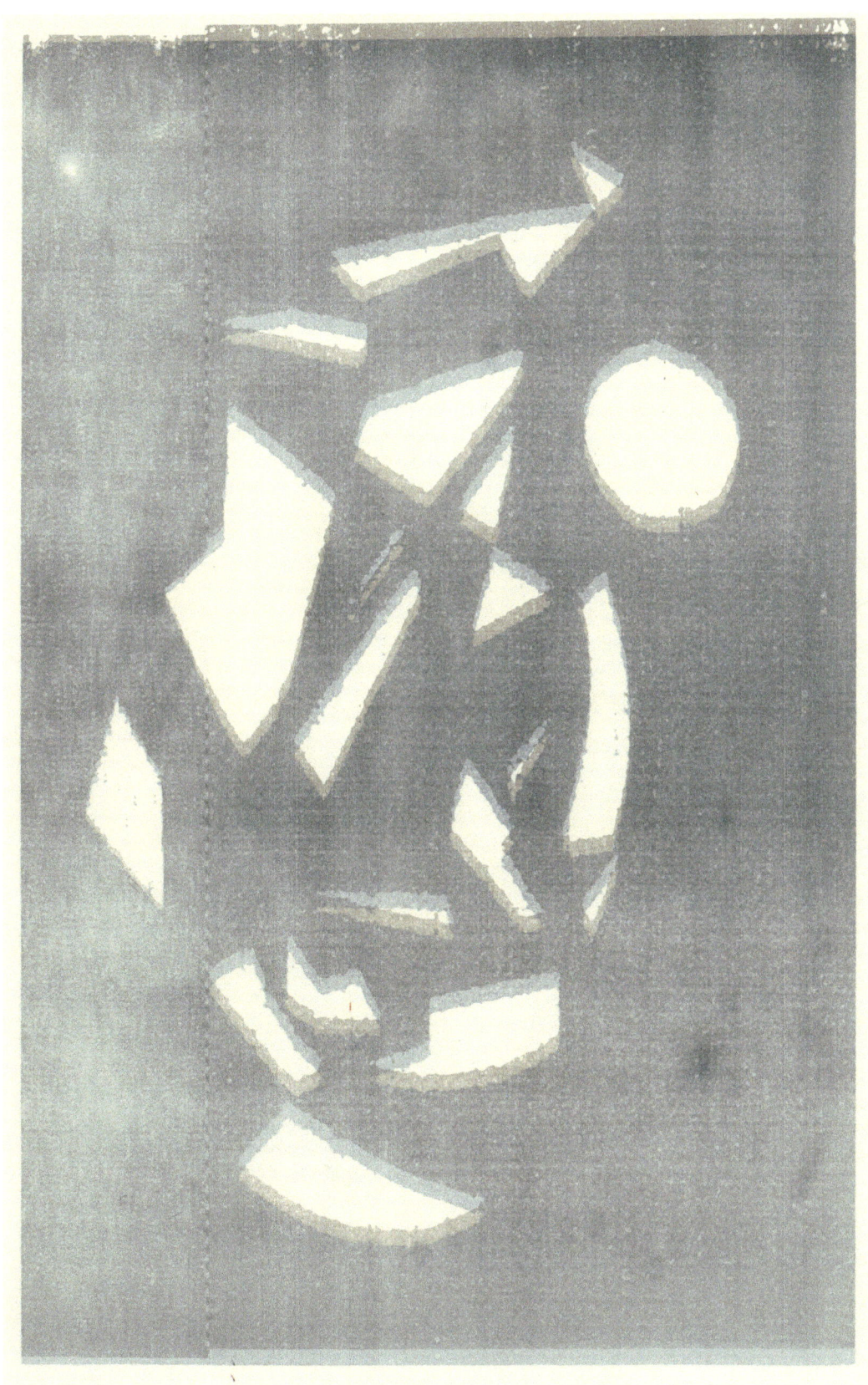

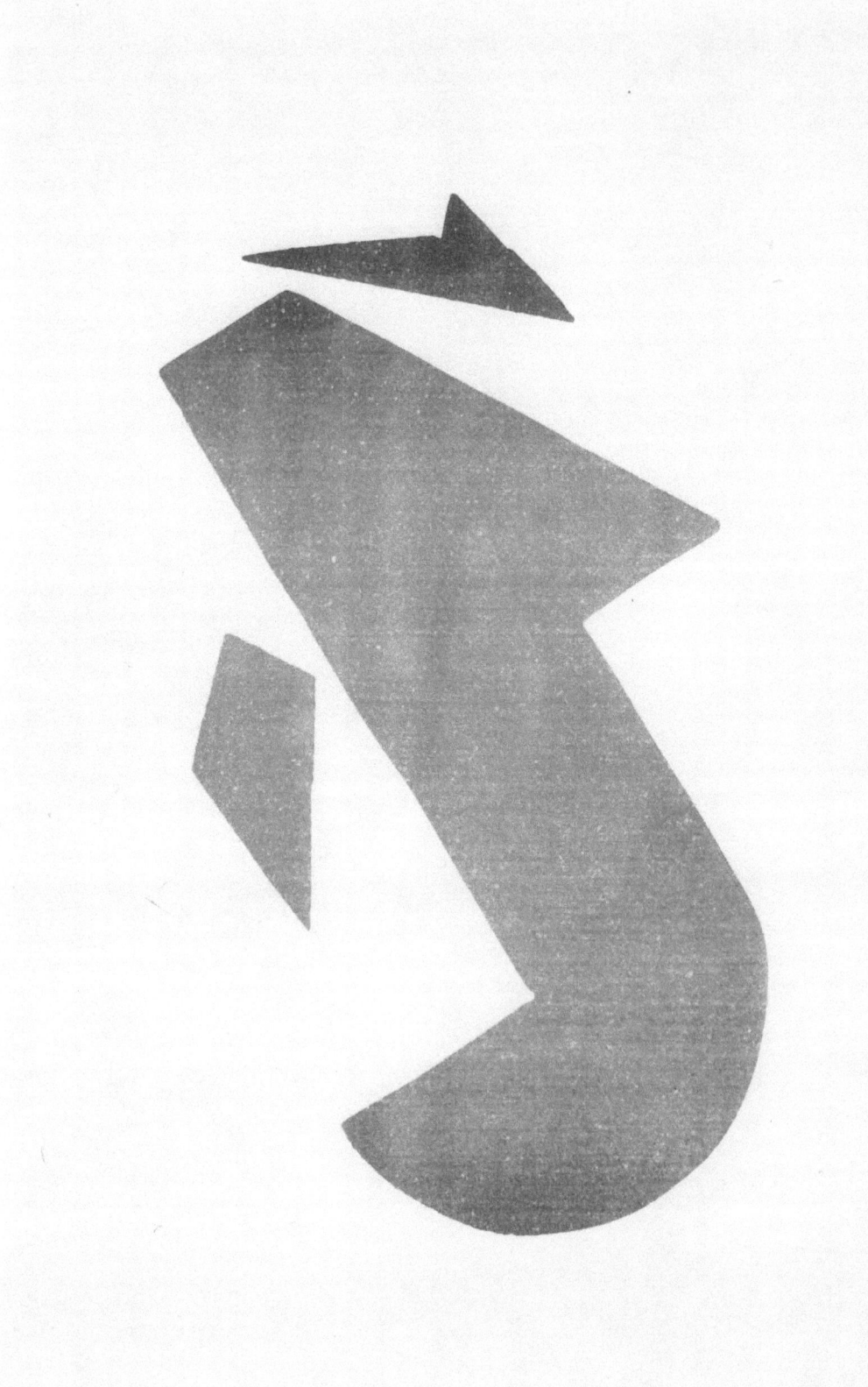

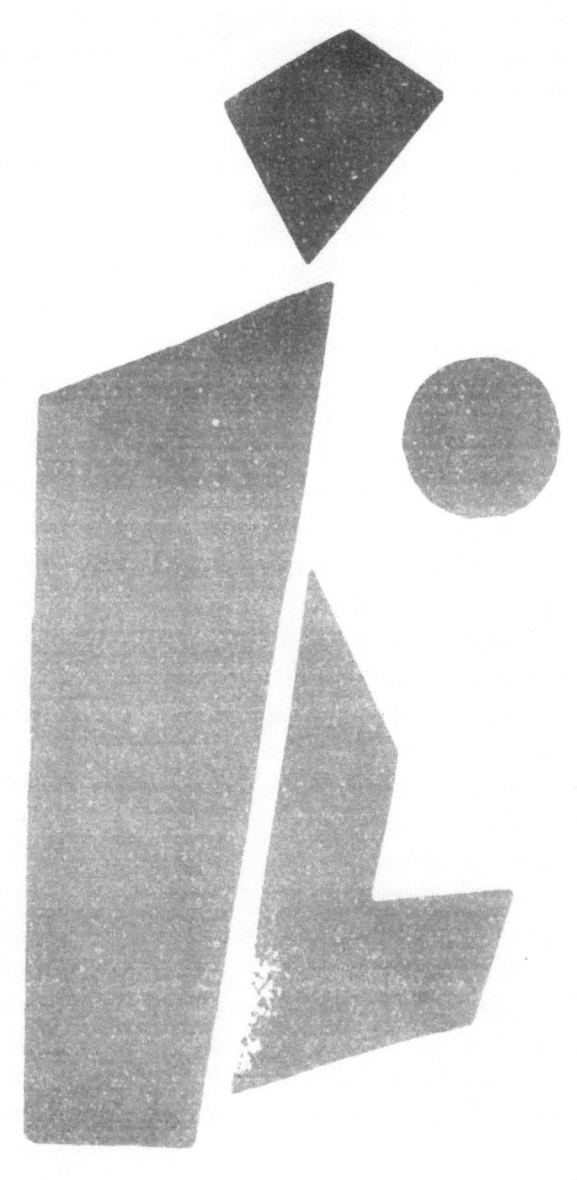

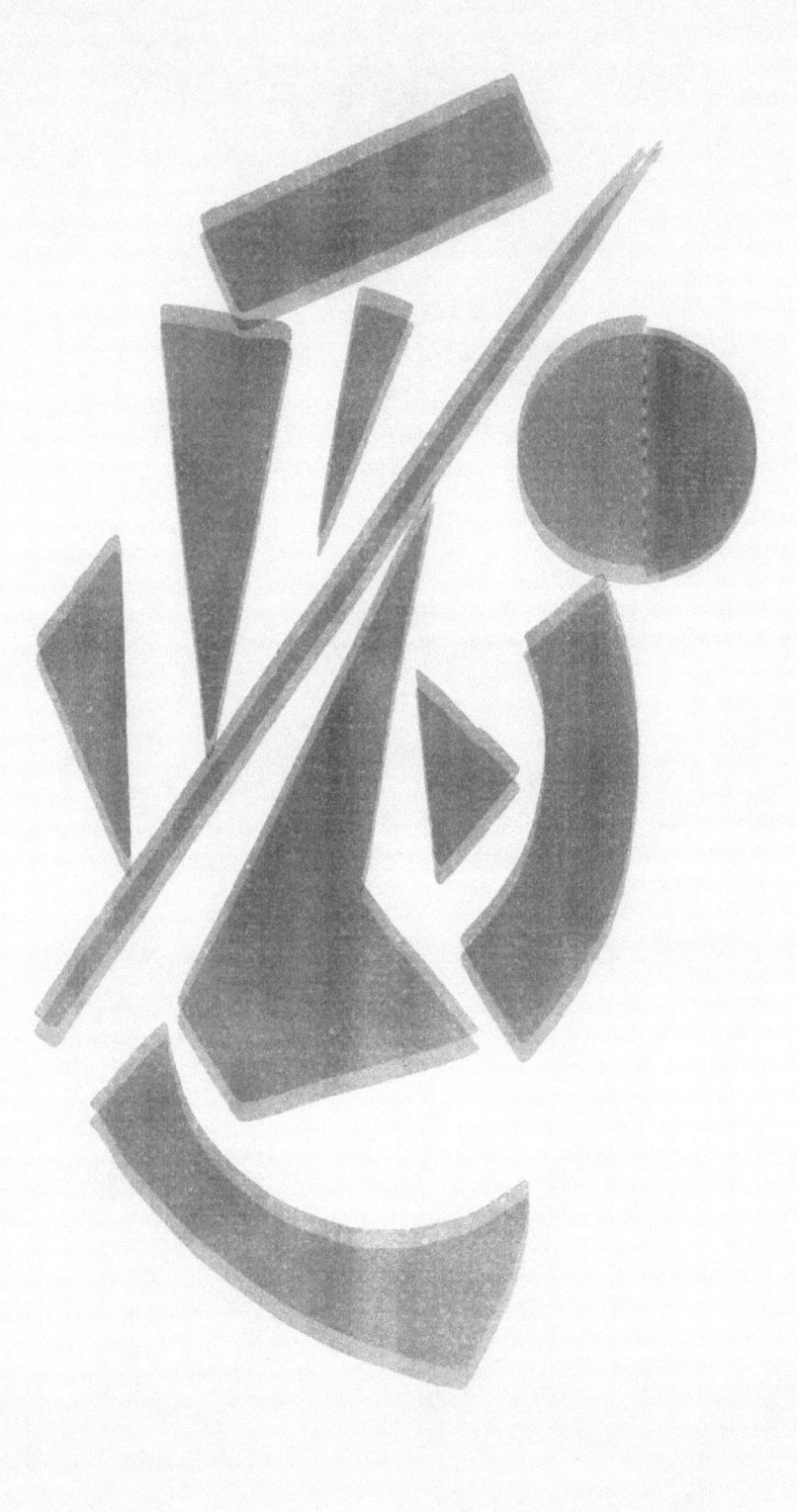

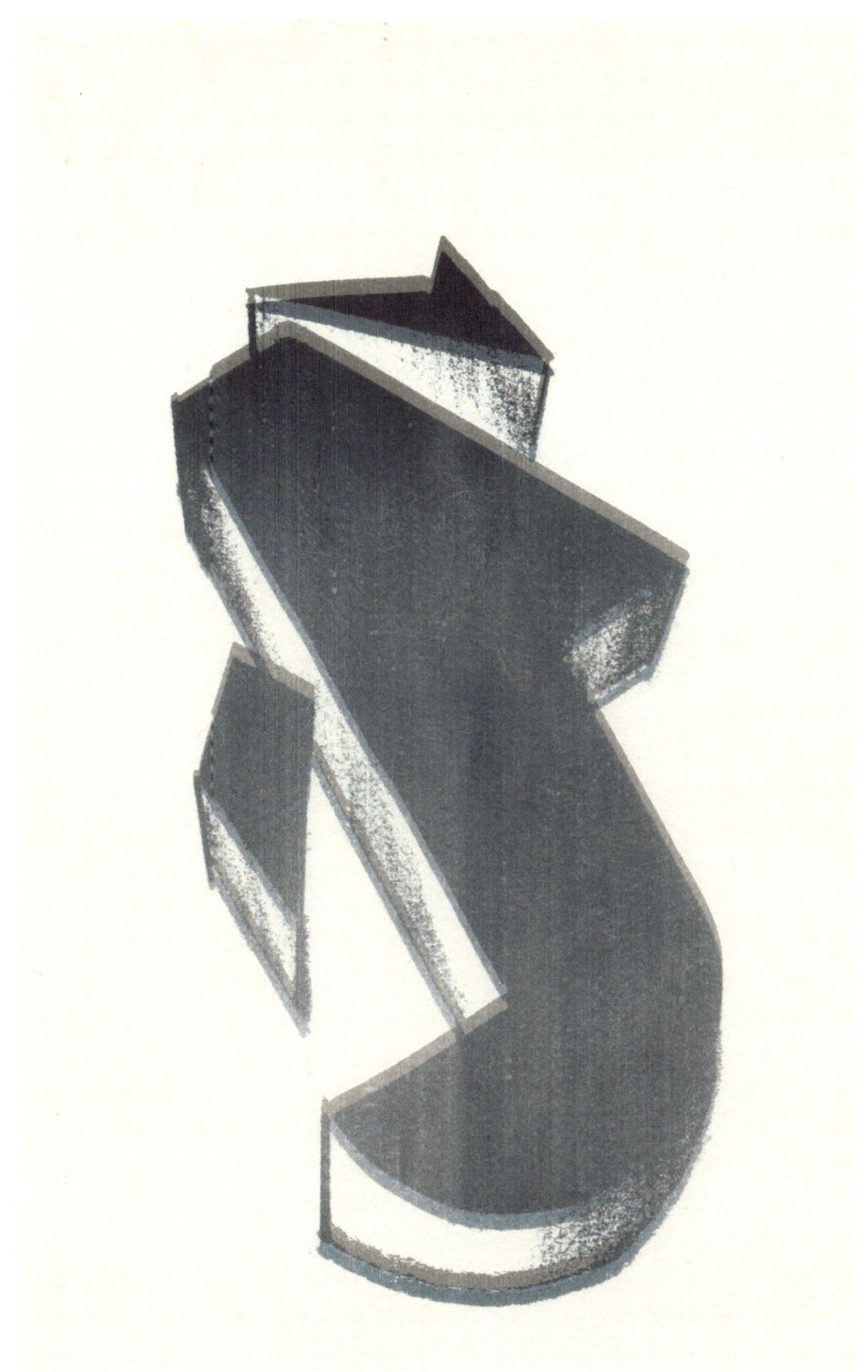

MATERIALS

Blocks may be of wood or linoleum and should be approximately seven-eights of an inch high. They can be engraved or cut with gouges or a knife. Printing inks bought from a reliable manufacturer are best. Permanent colors should be chosen. Artists' oil colors can be added in small quantities to the printing ink for additional colors that may not be obtainable in printers' inks.

Colors are applied to the block with a brayer or composition roller. Hard rubber rollers often advertised for this purpose are not as satisfactory as are the kind used by printers.

Japanese or Chinese paper of medium weight is the best, although there is an American paper of similar quality that can be used successfully.

Any press usually employed for printing type or other type-high material is best for making proofs. These usually have a registry guide for getting the colors to register properly.

The chip board referred to is a thin, uncoated board that is easily cut and sanded for texture and value variations. Regular carbon paper is to be used for transferring the tracing to the block.

EXPLANATION OF DIAGRAMS

The diagrams shown on the following pages represent some effects made possible through the use of simple materials. Also several means are illustrated for obtaining value changes. Any material can be used if the surface is relatively flat.

A—The straight line was cut with a knife and then scraped with the blade for a rough textural effect.

B—Curved lines were cut with a knife or razor blade and the value change effected by sanding the surface of the chip board.

C—Similar to B except that all lines were practically eliminated by sanding.

D—The slight change in value without confining lines was made by sanding with a fine grade of sand paper.

E—Was printed from a rough grade of artist's canvas.

F—Bristles were cut from a brush and arranged on a surface that had been coated with glue, and a piece of thin paper placed over this to hold the bristles in place.

G—Paper clips, held in place by transparent tape or glue.

H—String fastened to the chip board with glue.

All diagrams were printed in the following way. Color was applied to an unengraved linoleum block, the printing paper placed face down on this inked surface and the chip board, to which various materials had been attached, was placed over the paper and pressure applied, thus causing the transfer of the texture value or pattern to the paper.

The two center facing pages illustrate one way of getting correct registry of the different steps, beginning with the original sketch or drawing from which the finished print is being made and maintained in each successive step.

Diagram "important" shows how to establish the margins by use of a right angle corner formed by two pieces of wood slightly higher than a mounted piece of linoleum (approximately $\frac{3}{4}$ of an inch). All steps are fed to these registry marks indicated by the arrows, beginning with the original color drawing through to the final printing.

The diagram opposite "important" illustrates the necessity of keeping uniform margins or registry marks in all operations. Number one represents the drawing from which the print is being made; number two is the tracing made from the drawing and having the same margin as the drawing; number three represents make-ready of one color; number four represents the make-ready of another color; number five represents the printing paper and the block that carries the color. All of these must register; this is accomplished by the establishment of a margin and by keeping it uniform in all steps.

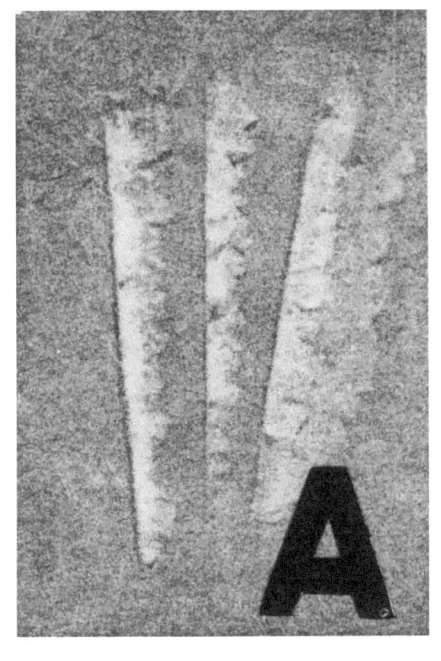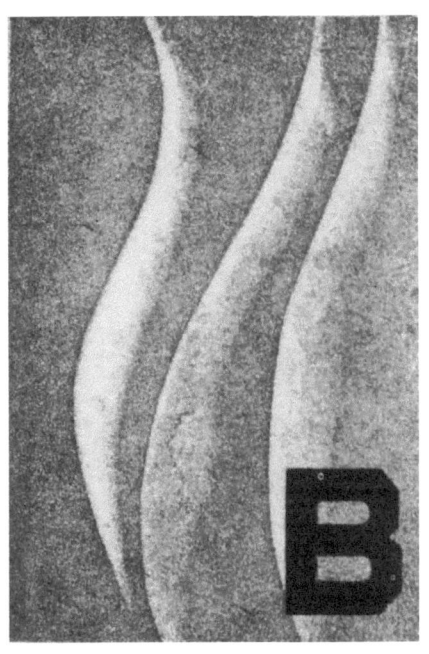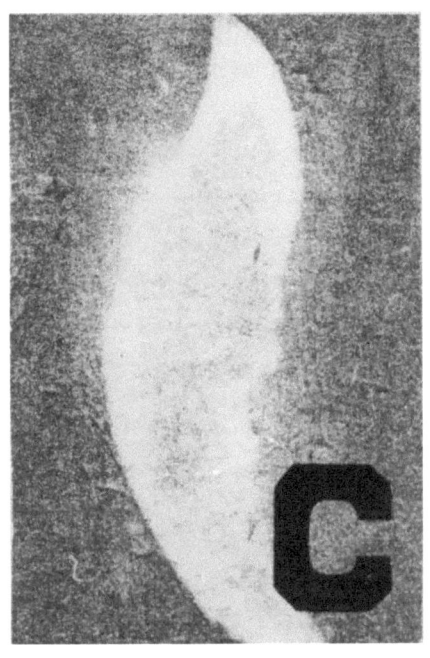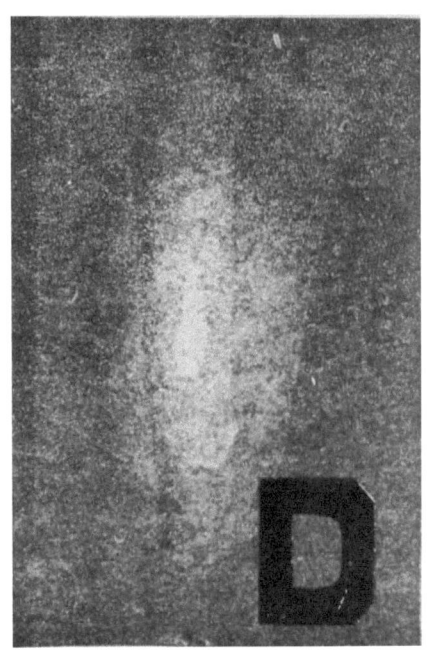

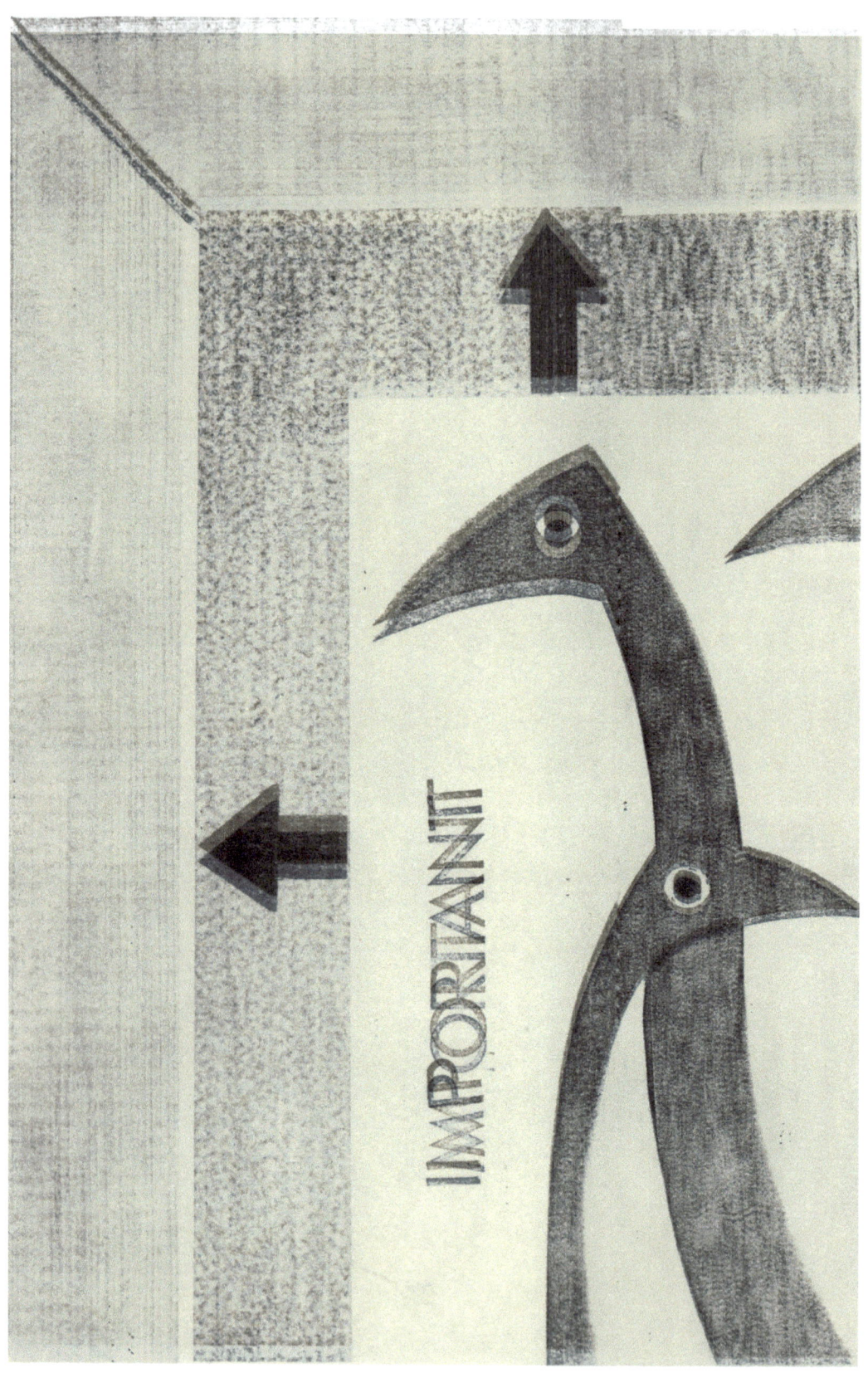

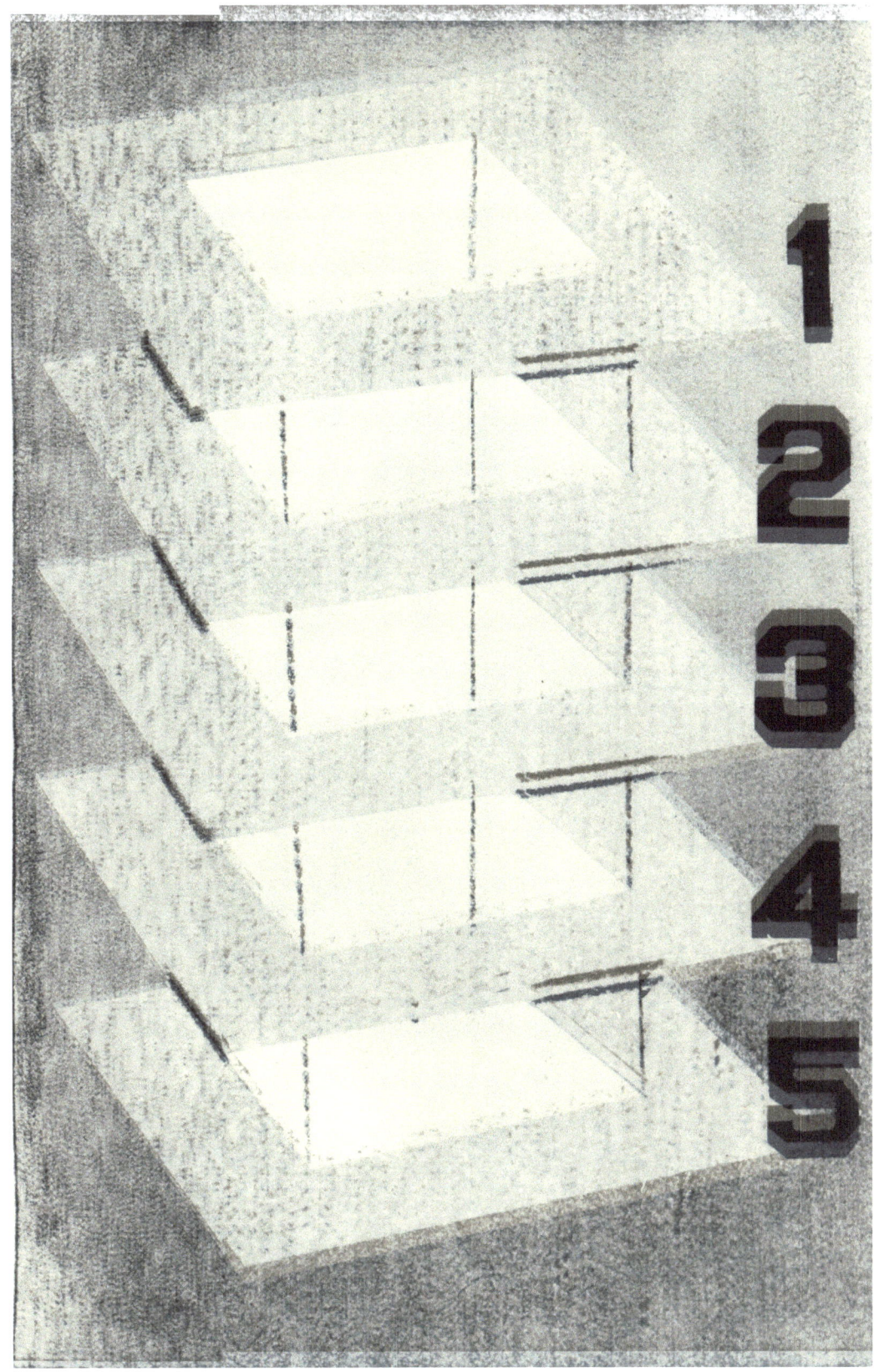

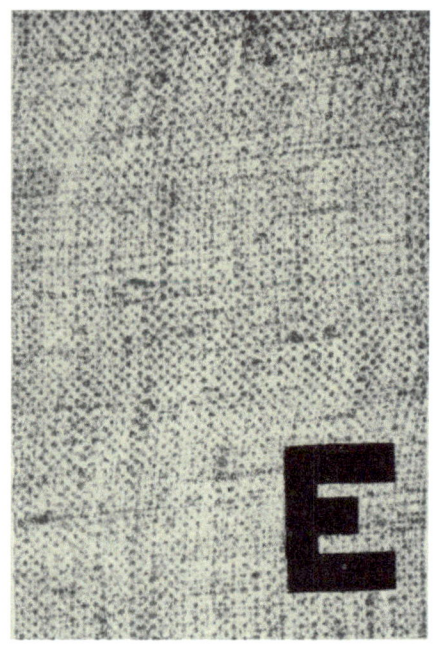
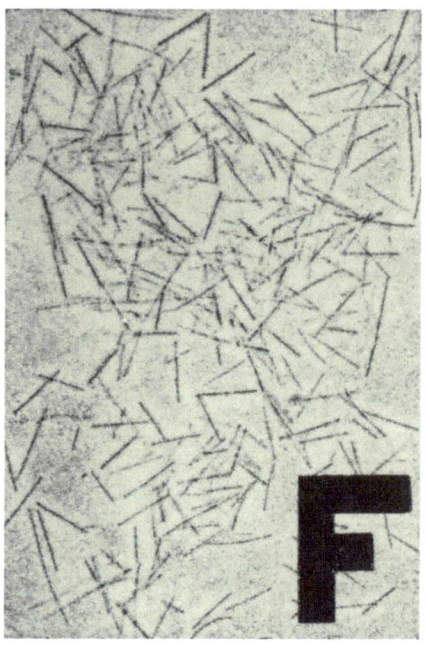
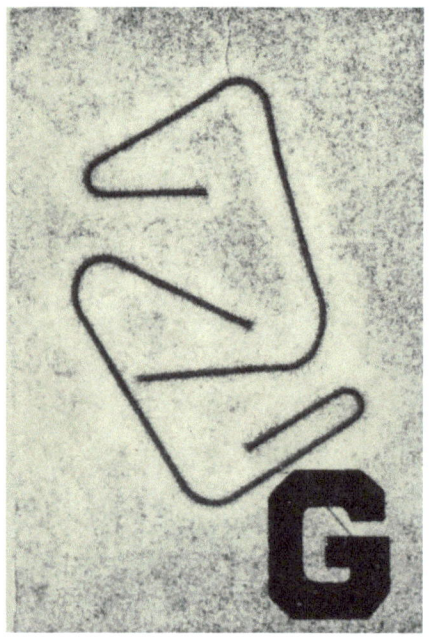
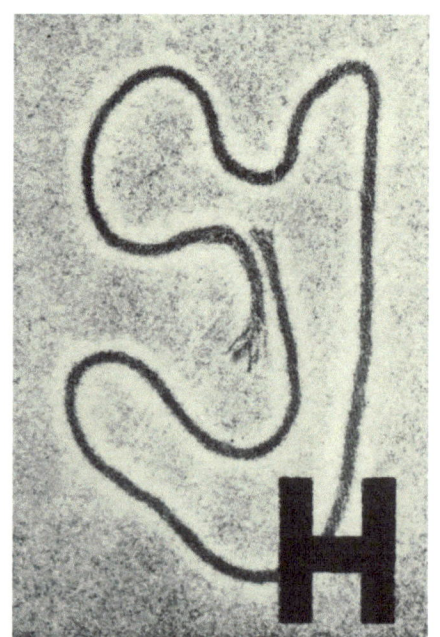

All of the color prints in this book were printed directly from hand-cut plates or from make-ready impressions. They were done on Japanese paper. The diagrams that follow each color print were done by a multilith process and are made directly from the make-ready impressions, or direct impressions as the case may be.

Three hundred copies of this book were printed at the University of Virginia Press in Charlottesville, Virginia in 1954.

Facsimile Edition
Published 2020
by Liber Apertus Press
Saratoga, California

Text and artwork reproduced
in high resolution at same size
as originally published

www.liberapertus.com
books@liberapertus.com

www.ingramcontent.com/pod-product-compliance
Lightning Source LLC
Chambersburg PA
CBHW051916210526
45473CB00006B/2036